At Issue

| Standardized Testing

Other Books in the At Issue Series:

At Issue

Standardized Testing

Diane Andrews Henningfeld, Book Editor

GREENHAVEN PRESS

An imprint of Thomson Gale, a part of The Thomson Corporation

Detroit • New York • San Francisco • New Haven, Conn. • Waterville, Maine • London

THOMSON

GALE

Christine Nasso, *Publisher*
Elizabeth Des Chenes, *Managing Editor*

© 2008 The Gale Group.

For more information, contact:
Greenhaven Press
27500 Drake Rd.
Farmington Hills, MI 48331-3535
Or you can visit our Internet site at http://www.gale.com

LIBRARY OF CONGRESS CATALOGING-IN-PUBLICATION DATA

Standardized testing / Roman Espejo, book editor.
   p. cm. -- (At issue)
  Includes bibliographical references and index.
  ISBN-13: 978-0-7377-3884-1 (hardcover)
  ISBN-13: 978-0-7377-3885-8 (pbk.)
  1. Educational tests and measurements--United States. I. Espejo, Roman, 1977-
  LB3051.S786 2008
  378.1'662--dc22

               2007032722

ISBN-10: 0-7377-3884-7 (hardcover)
ISBN-10: 0-7377-3885-5 (pbk.)

Printed in the United States of America
10 9 8 7 6 5 4 3 2 1

Contents

Introduction

Since it was signed on January 8, 2002, the No Child Left Behind Act (NCLB) has increased standardized testing in American schools. This federal law reactivated primary and secondary education programs that enforce standards of accountability for teachers, schools, districts, and states, using standardized testing as a chief assessment tool. As of July 2007, students' mathematics and reading skills are tested annually from the third to the eighth grade and once in high school. By the end of the 2007–2008 academic year, students will also be required to take a science test once in elementary school, middle school, and high school.

Standardized testing for accountability, or high-stakes testing, has significant consequences. Schools or school districts that do not meet adequate yearly progress (AYP) toward their state's proficiency goals must take numerous actions. For instance, schools that fail to meet AYP for two consecutive years must give eligible students the opportunity to attend intensive tutoring programs or transfer to high-performing schools by providing scholarships. If they routinely underperform on high-stakes tests, schools may also face restructuring and be required to make substantial changes in faculty or staff. Federal funding may be withheld as well. On the other hand, high-performing schools and states that make notable progress may receive rewards and bonuses; the NCLB Blue Ribbon Program, for example, recognizes low-performing schools that dramatically improve student performance. Teachers whose students score well on high-stakes tests may receive a promotion or bonus.

Because of the possible sanctions and punishments for low student performance and rewards and recognitions for high student performance, there have been cases in which teachers and schools have cheated on high-stakes testing. For example, at one time, California offered $25,000 bonuses for teachers at low-performing schools whose students showed the greatest test score improvements but retracted them due to cheating teachers. Furthermore, in 2003, dozens of schools in Texas were investigated for cheating on Texas Assessment of Knowledge and Skills (TAKS) tests. Two chronically low-performing schools in particular, Sanderson Elementary School in Houston and Harrell Budd Elementary school in Dallas, showed extreme score fluctuations that placed some of their students on par with students from the best schools in the state in just one year, leading to investigations that turned up evidence of organized cheating at both schools.

Some experts allege that the pressures of high-stakes testing create a climate of cheating. According to Robert Schaeffer, public education director at the National Center for Fair and Open Testing, "When test scores are all that matter, teachers, principals, and students will get their results by hook or by crook. When their job or future depend on one thing, people do unethical, irrational, and illegal things." Cheating occurs when teachers or other school personnel change incorrect answers on tests before they are electronically scored, give correct answers to students during testing, or allow students extra time to complete tests.

Though cheating does happen among educators, other experts contend that "suspicious" scores do not automatically indicate that a teacher or school cheated on high-stakes tests. Government professor Brian Jacob and economics and social studies professor Steven D. Levitt published a study on teacher and school cheating in 2004. They found that "mere fluctuations in test scores are not enough to justify an investigation into potential cheating. Evidence that students' answers may have been influenced by school personnel in an unethical manner is also necessary." Moreover, Jacob and Levitt also conclude that cheating in high-stakes testing, overall, is not a serious problem:

While evidence of cheating is sometimes used to impugn high-stakes testing programs, our results actually show that explicit cheating by school personnel is not likely to be a serious enough problem by itself to call into question high-stakes testing, both because the most egregious forms of cheating are relatively rare and, more important, because cheating could be virtually eliminated at a relatively low cost through the implementation of proper safeguards, such as those used by the Educational Testing Service on the SAT or GRE exams.

Cheating among teachers in high-stakes testing and the condoning of it in schools is just one of the numerous issues that surround the standardized testing controversy, which has gained more importance in recent years due to the revision of the SAT and possible renewal of NCLB in 2007. In *At Issue: Standardized Testing*, authors, experts, and professionals debate the validity of today's standardized tests as accurate, fair, and reliable measures of achievement and whether or not they have a justifiable place in the American educational system.

Standardized Testing Is Useful

Stephen G. Sireci

Stephen G. Sireci is a psychometrician, professor in the Research and Evaluation Methods Program, and director of the Center for Educational Assessment in the School of Education at the University of Massachusetts, Amherst.

Standardized testing faces wide opposition because it is part of student requirements for eligibility and advancement, and is used in accountability assessments that may negatively impact teachers, schools, or districts. However, the appropriate use of well-developed standardized tests is valuable toward continuous assessment, development, and improvement of curriculum and classroom instruction. Standardized testing allows schools to quickly adapt to new educational practices and ensures that teachers follow an approved curriculum framework. Concerns about the limitations of standardized tests are valid, but educators, policymakers, advocates, and researchers should work to improve—not reject—testing.

Tests are given for many reasons in the educational system. Many of these reasons are hated. For example, tests are major components in accountability systems that may have undesirable consequences for teachers, schools, or districts. Tests are also sometimes used as a requirement for something, such as high school graduation, scholarship, or eligibility to participate in collegiate athletics. In these instances, tests are often seen as a hurdle to overcome or as an unnecessary road-

Stephen G. Sireci, Ph.D, "In Defense of Testing: Are Educational Tests Inherently Evil?" *NERA Researcher*, February 2007. Reproduced by permission.

block to an inherent right. Tests are also commonly used to assign grades to students, particularly beyond elementary school. Given these purposes, who could possibly like tests? The answer is hardly anyone, perhaps only the relatively few high achievers who enjoy a challenge or the opportunity to show what they (we?) can do.

Why are tests so widespread if they are so hated? Is it the same reason we have intelligent design and global warming? Of course not. The reason is that educational tests, if developed carefully, used properly, and interpreted appropriately, have enormous utility. As soon as all sides of the educational community acknowledge that fact, we can make progress toward a common goal of using assessments to improve student learning.

To properly understand educational tests, particularly their benefits and limitations, we must consider their use in specific situations. In this [viewpoint], I discuss common perceptions and misconceptions of educational tests and the role tests currently play in federal and state education reform efforts. A primary goal of this discussion is to bridge the gap between proponents and opponents of standardized testing so that we can work together to improve student learning.

Standardized tests are one of the few, albeit incomplete, ways to measure outcomes of teaching.

Why Are Tests So Ubiquitous in Education?

A popular, but incorrect, myth is that educational [tests] are pushed by the extreme right of the political spectrum. This perception is simply false. Although the No Child Left Behind Act (NCLB) was proposed and signed by "he-who-must-not-be-named," [President George Bush] it was really an extension of [former president Bill] Clinton's *Goals 2000: Educate America* legislation, which was an extension of he-who-must-not-be-named's father's *America 2000* legislation. Thus, educational reform and accountability movements involving testing are one of the few bipartisan areas of legislation we have seen over the past several decades. There are, of course, strong differences in educational policy between Democrats and Republicans, such as the *financing* of education, but it is important to note that the NCLB Act was sponsored by Democrat Ted Kennedy and Republican Judd Gregg in the Senate and Democrat George Miller and Republican John Boehner in the House. It passed overwhelmingly in both (87–10 in the Senate and 381–41 in the House).

Why do federal legislators agree that mandated testing is an important part of education reform? There are several reasons. First, assessment is seen as a critical component in the educational process. In fact, quality education requires continuous interaction among instruction, curriculum, and assessment. Good instruction starts with good curricula and both influence each other. The development of curricula at the district and state levels is certainly influenced by what teachers teach in their classrooms. As the curricula are developed, teaching practices change accordingly. Assessments are needed to discover what students are learning. Based on that information, changes to instruction and curricula occur. . . .

A second reason tests play a prominent role in federal and state education reform movements is that they are an effective means for quickly changing instructional practices. As [author Lorraine M.] McDonnell described "although standardized tests are primarily measurement tools to obtain information about student and school performance, they are also strategies for pursuing a variety of political goals". McDonnell also points out that there are few alternatives available to policy makers to enforce their educational policies. As she put it "Testing's strong appeal is largely attributable to the lack of alternative policy strategies that fit the unique circumstances of public schooling. . . . Standardized tests are one of the few, albeit incomplete, ways to measure outcomes of teaching".

A third reason mandated testing is a key component of education reform is that it forces educators to align their instruction with state curriculum frameworks. No teacher likes to be overly constrained regarding what she or he should teach. However, no one wants teachers spending large amounts of instructional time teaching knowledge and skills that most would consider unimportant, relative to other skills. Thus, education involves consensus about what should be taught. The development of curriculum frameworks without a means for assessing how well students master the objectives within them would create a situation in which the good work done in developing the frameworks could be simply ignored.

Critics of state-mandated testing argue that these tests narrow the curriculum and force teaching-to-the-test. Proponents counter that the tests are aligned with curriculum frameworks, which were developed through a consensus process, and so teaching to the test is teaching to the frameworks. As in most debates, the truth probably lies somewhere in the middle. Nevertheless, it is important to bear in mind that the idea behind consensus statewide curriculum frameworks and tests designed to measure them is a noble one, because its goal is to improve instruction. As a parent, I can understand this position. After all, I want to know that my sons' teachers are teaching the important knowledge and skills they will need to succeed personally and academically. State curriculum frameworks and tests designed to measure them attempt to ensure that what is taught is important. . . .

Focusing on Test Use

One of the greatest challenges we experience as educational researchers is asking the right research questions. With respect to educational testing, the questions we ask should be specific to using a test for a particular purpose. Thus, questions motivating research in this area should not be "Is the test bad?" or "Is the test fair?" but rather "Will the results of this test provide the information it is designed to produce?" Thus, evaluating a test means evaluating the use of a test for a particular purpose. Tests are not inherently "good" or inherently "bad," but using a test for some purpose could be either, depending on what the test was designed to do versus what it is used for. This notion is clear in the definition of *validity* presented in the *Standards for Educational and Psychological Testing*:

> Validity refers to the degree to which evidence and theory support the interpretations of test scores entailed by proposed uses of tests.

As is evident in this definition, it is not a test that is validated per se, but the use of a test for a particular purpose. Defending inferences derived from test scores involves both qualitative evidence based on theories of what is being measured and quantitative evidence indicating the scores reflect the measured attribute. Thus, all educational researchers can contribute to research on testing, regardless of their particular research orientation. I will not discuss specific means for validating inferences in this column. Instead, I focus on test use in educational testing and how it can help or hurt the educational process.

Teachers who are not helping our students reach their academic potential are much more dangerous to our children than any test.

How are tests used in education? Teachers use tests to measure how well students grasp the material taught (e.g., classroom tests). Counselors use tests to diagnose students' strengths and weaknesses and make referrals for remediation, advanced courses, or other placement decisions. Policy makers use tests to evaluate teachers, schools, districts, states, countries, and various educational programs. Tests are also used as one criterion for high school graduation and for other types of certification such as an honors diploma, and for admissions into postsecondary and graduate education. As the stakes associated with educational tests increase, such as in the cases of granting a high school diploma or evaluating the performance of particular teachers, the criticisms also increase. And they should increase. If a test is used to make a "big" decision, the use of the test for that purpose should be supported by "big" evidence. Thus, as educational researchers, our assessment research activities should be focused on asking the right questions about test use (e.g., Is there evidence to support use of this test as a high school graduation requirement?).

I am a psychometrician working in educational measurement and so it is pretty obvious that I must believe in the usefulness of educational tests. However, my strong belief in the utility of educational tests stems not from my psychometric training, but from my experience as a parent. How do I know if my sons are receiving a good education? The class work, assignments, and report cards that come home give me some indication, but the norm-referenced and criterion-referenced test score reports give me a lot more to go on. The Iowa Tests of Basic Skills that our local school district uses allows me to compare my sons' performance to national norms. The Massachusetts Comprehensive Assessment System (MCAS) tests allow me to see how my sons are doing with respect to the performance standards established by the State. Now, when my wife and I speak with their teachers or the principal, we can talk about these independent assessments, and how this information can be used to improve their instruction.

Looking Forward: Collaborating on Educational Assessment Research

In this [viewpoint], I merely touched on a few of the important issues that concern educational assessment policy and the proper use of tests in our nation's schools. I know there are many people who will never acknowledge the utility of a standardized test, but I also know there are many more who hate something else—bad teaching! Teachers who are not helping our students reach their academic potential are much more dangerous to our children than any test. I do not advocate using tests to "police" teachers or using test results to provide sanctions and rewards for teachers (a very bad idea, given the different types of students taught by different teachers). However, I like the idea of measuring students' achievement with respect to standards developed through a consensus process, and I like the idea of providing as much information as possible to parents and others about the academic achievement and progress of their children.

Are there problems with our current educational assessment policies? I think so. There are several valid criticisms about current educational tests. Personally, I am concerned about the amount our students are tested, and I am very concerned about the pressure that is put on students before they take a test. So, there is much room for improvement, which is where we, as educational researchers, come in. Let us not throw the baby out with the bathwater and simply dismiss tests as useless. Instead, let us research what seems to be working, what seems to be harmful, and what needs to be improved. By working together, we can improve educational assessment and provide advice to educational policy makers that is based on solid research. If we can do that, we will improve curriculum development, instruction, and assessment, with the happy consequence of improving student learning.

2

Standardized Testing
Has Serious Limitations

FairTest: The National Center for Fair and Open Testing

FairTest: The National Center for Fair and Open Testing is an organization that advocates for the reform of current standardized testing and assessment practices in education and employment.

Standardized testing should not be used as the primary tool to assess students' knowledge, progress, and abilities; maintain school and district accountability; shape curriculum and classroom instruction; and make eligibility, advancement, and admissions decisions. Such examinations do not test creativity or complex thinking skills, rely on largely irrelevant state standards, and are not objective measures of student ability or achievement. Comprehensive classroom-based assessments, on the contrary, can provide more meaningful insight on students and the quality of their curriculum and instruction than narrow and unreliable multiple-choice exams.

Standardized tests have historically been used as measures of how students compare with each other (norm-referenced) or how much of a particular curriculum they have learned (criterion-referenced). Increasingly, standardized tests are being used to make major decisions about students, such as grade promotion or high school graduation, and schools. More and more often, they also are intended to shape curriculum and instruction.

FairTest: The National Center for Fair and Open Testing, "FairTest Fact Sheets: 'The Limits of Standardized Testing for Diagnosing and Assisting Student Learning' and 'What's Wrong with Standardized Tests?'" *FairTest (www.fairtest.org)*, Reproduced by permission.

Proponents of the expanded uses and consequences of tests claim that newer exams are superior to the flawed exams of the past, measure what is important, and are worth teaching to. These arguments ignore the real-world limits to what standardized tests can usefully do. Repeating such false claims perpetuates test misuse and the dangerous belief that what is worth teaching is that which can be assessed by a standardized test.

Under a new federal law, state assessments of reading and math must be administered for accountability annually in grades 3–8 and once in high schools. The assessments must be based on state content and performance standards; measure higher order thinking; provide useful diagnostic information; and be valid and reliable. While the law does not mandate the use of standardized tests, many states will be inclined [to] administer them to meet the federal law. An examination of each requirement, however, reveals the limits of standardized tests.

Standardized exams offer few opportunities to display the attributes of higher-order thinking, such as analysis, synthesis, evaluation, and creativity.

Tests Are To Be Based on State Standards

State standards are often too long and detailed to ever be taught. Many fail to distinguish what is important from what is unimportant or to separate what all students ought to learn in a subject from what only the most interested might learn. In part because of the level of detail, much of the content in state standards is not assessed by state tests.

Moreover, much of value in state standards cannot be tested with any paper-and-pencil test of a few hours duration. In a high quality education, students conduct science experiments, solve real-world math problems, write research papers, read novels and stories and analyze them, make oral presentations, evaluate and synthesize information from a variety of fields, and apply their learning to new and ill-defined situations. Standardized tests are poor tools for evaluating these important kinds of learning. If instruction focuses on the test, students will not learn these skills, which are needed for success in college and often in life.

Measure Higher-Order Thinking

Standardized exams offer few opportunities to display the attributes of higher-order thinking, such as analysis, synthesis, evaluation, and creativity. Higher order thinking is encouraged and revealed by in-depth and extended work, not by one-shot tests.

Provide Useful Diagnostic Information

Assessments of educational strengths and weaknesses can be useful at the individual, classroom, school or district levels. However, information needs to be sufficiently timely, accurate, meaningful, detailed and comprehensive for the kind of diagnosis being made. The lengthy turn-around time for scoring most standardized tests makes them nearly useless for helping a particular individual, though the information might be of some value to teachers and schools for longer-range planning.

To improve learning and provide meaningful accountability, schools and districts cannot rely solely on standardized tests.

In addition, standardized tests usually include only a few questions on any particular topic. This is too little information to produce accurate, comprehensive or detailed results. Many topics in state standards are not addressed at all in state exams, so the tests provide no diagnostic information about them.

Diagnosis suggests the use of "formative" assessment—assessments that can help a teacher and student know what to do next. Standardized tests administered at the end of the year—"summative assessment"—cannot possibly meet this need. Sound diagnostic practices also include understanding why a student is having difficulty or success and determining appropriate action. As snapshots with limited information, standardized tests provide neither an answer to "why" nor little guidance for successful instruction.

Be Valid and Reliable

Test validity, experts explain, resides in the inferences drawn from assessment results and the consequences of their uses. Relying solely on scores from one test to determine success or progress in broad areas such as reading or math is likely to lead to incorrect inferences and then to actions that are ineffective or even harmful. For these and other reasons, the standards of the testing profession call for using multiple measures for informing major decisions—as does the ESEA [Elementary and Secondary Education Act] legislation.

Reliability, or consistency of information, is sometimes treated as the most important aspect of testing. However, consistent information about too narrow a range of topics, skills or knowledge cannot provide adequate information for credible decisions: a doctor needs more than just reliable blood pressure results to treat a patient. Well-designed classroom-based assessments can provide richer, consistent information that enhances validity, diagnostic capacity, and the ability to assess progress toward meaningful standards.

Inherent Limits

When standardized tests are the primary factor in accountability, the temptation is to use the tests to define curriculum and focus instruction. What is not tested is not taught, and what is taught does not include higher-order learning. How the subject is tested becomes a model for how to teach the subject. At the extreme, school becomes a test prep program—and this extreme already exists.

It is of course possible to use a standardized test and not let its limits control curriculum and instruction. However, this can result in a school putting itself at risk for producing lower test scores. It also means parents and the community are not informed systematically about the non-tested areas, unless the school or district makes a great effort.

[A]n individual's score may vary from day to day due to testing conditions or the test-taker's mental or emotional state.

To improve learning and provide meaningful accountability, schools and districts cannot rely solely on standardized tests. The inherent limits of the instruments allow them only to generate information that is inadequate in both breadth and depth. Thus, states, districts and schools must find ways to strengthen classroom assessments and to use the information that comes from these richer measures to inform the public.

What's wrong with standardized tests? Are standardized tests fair and helpful evaluation tools? Not really. Standardized tests are tests on which all students answer the same questions, usually in multiple-choice format, and each question has only one correct answer. They reward the ability to quickly answer superficial questions that do not require real thought. They do not measure the ability to think or create in any field. Their use encourages a narrowed curriculum, outdated methods of instruction, and harmful practices such as retention in grade and tracking. They also assume all test-takers have been exposed to a white, middle-class background.

Are standardized tests objective? The only objective part of most standardized tests is the scoring, when it is done by machine. What items to include on the test, the wording and content of the items, the determination of the "correct" answer, choice of test, how the test is administered, and the uses of the results are all decisions made by subjective human beings.

Are test scores "reliable"? A test is completely reliable if you would get exactly the same results the second time you administered it. All existing tests have "measurement error." This means an individual's score may vary from day to day due to testing conditions or the test-taker's mental or emotional state. As a result, many individuals' scores are frequently wrong. Test scores of young children and scores on subsections of tests are much less reliable than test scores on adults or whole tests.

Classroom surveys show teachers do not find scores from standardized tests very helpful, so they rarely use them.

Do test scores reflect real differences among people? Not necessarily. To construct a norm-referenced test (a test on which half the test-takers score above average, the other half below), test makers must make small differences among people appear large. Because item content differs from one test to another, even tests that claim to measure the same thing often produce very different results. Because of measurement error, two people with very different scores on one test administration might get the same scores on a second administration. On the [old] SAT, for example, the test-makers admit that two students' scores must differ by at least 144 points (out of 1600) before they are willing to say the students' measured abilities really differ.

Don't test-makers remove bias from test? Most test-makers review items for obvious biases, such as offensive words. But this is inadequate, since many forms of bias are not superficial. Some test-makers also use statistical bias-reduction techniques. However, these techniques cannot detect underlying bias in the test's form or content. As a result, biased cultural assumptions built into the test as a whole are not exposed or removed by test-makers.

Do IQ tests measure intelligence? IQ tests assume that intelligence is one thing that can be easily measured and put on a scale, rather than a variety of abilities. They also assume intelligence is fixed and permanent. However, psychologists cannot agree whether there is one thing that can be called intelligence, or whether it is fixed, let alone meaningfully measure "it." Studies have shown that IQ scores can be changed by training, nutrition, or simply by having more friendly people administer the test. In reality, IQ tests are nothing more than a type of achievement test which primarily measures knowledge of standard English and exposure to the cultural experiences of middle class whites.

Do tests reflect what we know about how students learn? No. Standardized tests are based in behaviorist psychological theories from the nineteenth century. While our understanding of the brain and how people learn and think has progressed enormously, tests have remained the same. Behaviorism assumed that knowledge could be broken into separate bits and that people learned by passively absorbing these bits. Today, cognitive and developmental psychologists understand that knowledge is not separable bits and that people (including children) learn by connecting what they already know with what they are trying to learn. If they cannot actively make meaning out of what they are doing, they do not learn or remember. But most standardized tests do not incorporate the modern theories and are still based on recall of isolated facts and narrow skills.

Do multiple-choice tests measure important student achievement? Multiple-choice tests are a very poor yardstick of student performance. They do not measure the ability to write, to use math, to make meaning from text when reading, to understand scientific methods or reasoning, or to grasp social science concepts. Nor do these tests adequately measure thinking skills or assess what people can do on real-world tasks.

Are test scores helpful to teachers? Standardized, multiple choice tests were not originally designed to provide help to teachers. Classroom surveys show teachers do not find scores from standardized tests very helpful, so they rarely use them. The tests do not provide information that can help a teacher understand what to do next in working with a student because they do not indicate how the student learns or thinks. Good evaluation would provide helpful information to teachers.

Are readiness or screening tests helpful? Readiness tests, used to determine if a child is ready for school, are very inaccurate and unsound. They encourage overly academic, developmentally inappropriate primary schooling. Screening tests for disabilities are often not adequately validated; they also promote a view of children as having deficits to be corrected, rather than having individual differences and strengths on which to build.

Are there better ways to evaluate student achievement or ability? Yes. Good teacher observation, documentation of student work, and performance-based assessment, all of which involve the direct evaluation of student effort on real learning tasks, provide useful material for teachers, parents, the community and the government.

3

Minorities Support Standardized Testing

Jonathan Zimmerman

Jonathan Zimmerman is director of the history of education program at the Steinhardt School of Education at New York University. He is also author of Whose America?: Culture Wars in the Public School.

One of the main objections against standardized testing is that it discriminates against minorities, particularly black Americans and Latinos. Yet numerous public opinion surveys show that these minorities strongly support standardized testing. Black American and Latino parents favor discipline and strong curriculum in the classroom to raise standardized test scores, especially for students who live in violent neighborhoods and unstable homes. Nonetheless, despite these prevailing views among black Americans and Latinos, educational reformers and various organizations continue to argue that standardized testing hinders minority achievement.

[In May 2005], a group called the New York Collective of Radical Educators staged a protest against standardized testing.

Responding to recent reports about substantial gains for fourth-graders on citywide reading and writing examinations, the group argued that the improved scores reflect "drill-and-kill" test-preparation activities rather than real learning. Worst of all, protesters maintained, the entire testing enterprise dis-

1

Jonathan Zimmerman, "Minorities Support 'Racist' Tests," *Christian Science Monitor*, June 2, 2005. www.csmonitor.com. Reproduced by permission of the author.

criminates against racial minorities. For blacks and Hispanics especially, they said, standardized tests inhibit academic achievement and increase the dropout rate.

The only problem is, blacks and Hispanics don't see it that way.

Over the past decade, public opinion surveys have demonstrated overwhelming support among racial minorities for high-stakes testing. In a 2003 study by the Pew Hispanic Center, for example, three-quarters of Latinos said that standardized tests "should be used to determine whether students are promoted or can graduate." Two-thirds agreed that the federal government "should require states to set strict performance standards for public schools," as mandated under President Bush's No Child Left Behind (NCLB) Act.

Likewise, African-Americans favor high-stakes tests by large margins. To be sure, activist groups like the National Association for the Advancement of Colored People have criticized NCLB and state graduation exams. But the black rank and file tell another story.

According to a 1998 survey by Public Agenda, nearly 8 of 10 African-American parents want schools to test children and publicize black-white achievement differences, just as NCLB requires. Only 28 percent say that standardized tests are "culturally biased" against black children, as critics often maintain. Many of these critics work at schools of education, where the standardized test serves as a symbol of everything that's wrong with American teaching.

The Ed-School Gospel

According to the Ed-School Gospel, as I call it, schools should reflect student interests, not the sterile demands of "the curriculum"; they should employ a wide variety of classroom materials, not just the district-approved textbook; they should promote group learning and cooperation, and they should evaluate each student based on her or his own progress, not on district or statewide norms.

In every way, the argument goes, standardized testing harms these goals. It ignores the interests of the individual student; it promotes needless competition and anxiety; it turns learning into a lock-step exercise, inhibiting exploration and imagination; and it measures students against an arbitrary standard, ignoring their idiosyncratic abilities and attributes.

As a professor at an American school of education, I share many of these concerns. But I also worry that the Ed-School Gospel blinds us to the concerns of American racial minorities, who simply don't see the world the way we do. They want classrooms that stress discipline, that follow a strict curriculum, and that help children succeed on—gasp—standardized tests.

Especially if students live in chaotic or dangerous home environments, minority parents argue, they need the order and structure of a traditional school.

That doesn't mean minority parents are right, of course. But it does mean that the people who run our schools—and, especially, our schools of education—need to take these opinions into account. We can no longer dismiss high-stakes testing as "racist" when so many racial minorities want it.

Unfortunately, we also have a rich tradition of ignoring popular sentiment. Even [educational reformer] John Dewey, the greatest tribune of modern American democracy and education, questioned whether citizens should influence school policy. "Are the schools doing what the people want them to do?" he asked in 1901.

"The schools are not doing, and cannot do," he continued, "what the people want until there is more unity, more definiteness, in the community's consciousness of its own needs; but it is the business of the school to forward this conception."

In other words, educators should tell the people what they really need. That's fine, so long as we listen to them as well.

Ed-school professors love to talk about "hearing the voices" of blacks and Hispanics, who are too often excluded from America's educational dialogues. But when minorities express an opinion that we don't like, we turn a deaf ear. That's a lousy model for education, and an even worse one for democracy.

Whatever we think of America's current testing craze, American racial minorities clearly endorse it. And if we dismiss their views out of hand, we'll be demeaning the very people whom we claim to defend.

4

Standardized Testing Is Racist

Harold Berlak

Harold Berlak is an independent researcher and consultant and has written extensively on issues of testing and assessment. He is also a fellow at the Educational Policy Research Unit, Arizona State University, Tempe. He is author-editor of Toward A New Science of Testing and Educational Assessment *(SUNY Press, 1992).*

Standardized testing perpetuates institutionalized racism and contributes to the achievement gap between whites and minorities. For instance, the deeply embedded stereotype that African Americans perform poorly on standardized tests hinders many African Americans' testing ability. Also, research has shown that minorities statistically have lower standardized test scores than whites because of existing, hidden biases in the development and administration of standardized tests and interpretation of their scores. Therefore, the achievement gap will not begin to close until current standards and assessment tests are significantly reformed.

That there is a race gap in educational achievement is not news. Large numbers of the nation's children leave school, with and without high school diplomas, barely able to read, write, and do simple math. But the failures of the school are not evenly distributed. They fall disproportionately on students of color.

Even when parents' income and wealth is comparable, African Americans, Native Americans, Latinos, and immigrants for whom English is not a first language lag behind English-speaking, native-born, white students. The evidence for the gap has been documented repeatedly by the usual measures. These include drop-out rates, relative numbers of students who take the advanced placement examination, who are enrolled in the top academic and "gifted" classes and/or admitted to higher-status secondary schools, colleges, graduate, and professional programs. And last but not least, are the discrepancies in scores on standardized tests of academic achievement, on which teachers' and students' fate so heavily depend. . . .

Historical Explantion

Over the years, the major reasons given for the claimed superior attainments of whites in cultural, artistic, and academic endeavors were overtly racist. It was said that the explanation lay in the superior genes of white northern European, Anglo-Americans. As the social sciences developed in the latter years of the 19th and the 20th centuries, "scientific" tracts defending white supremacy appeared with regularity. By the 1930's, the eugenics movement (which posited a biological basis for the superiority of whites) managed to gain a foothold in North American universities. And, it is relevant to add, all the leaders of this overtly racist movement were the leaders of the newly emerging field of scientific mental measurement. Many were the same men who testified before Congress in the early 1920's and lent scientific credence to the racist immigration exclusion acts which barred or greatly restricted immigration from Asia, Latin America, and southern and eastern Europe. The eugenics movement was considered a respectable academic discipline until it was discredited following the defeat of the Third Reich and the immensity of the crimes committed in the name of Nordic racial purity. . . .

Recently a more subtle form of "scientific" racism has gained some respectability. The inferiority of the Black and brown races is now said to lie not necessarily in genetics but in culture and history. This more quietly spoken academic version of the master-race ideology has also been thoroughly dismantled, yet racist explanations for the race gap persist.

Once all "scientific" arguments supporting racism are dismissed, how is the ever-present gap in academic school performance to be explained? Numerous social and behavioral scientists have addressed this question.

A statistical study by Professor Samuel Meyers Jr. at the Roy Wilkins Center for Human Relations and Social Justice at the University of Minnesota sought to determine whether poverty was a primary cause of the poor performance of Black students on the Minnesota Basic Standards Test. Passing this test was scheduled to become a prerequisite for a high school diploma in 2000. In a 1996 trial run in Minneapolis, 75 percent of African-American students failed the math test, and 79 percent failed in reading, compared to 26 percent and 42 percent respectively for whites.

African American students who were told that the test was a true measure of ability scored significantly lower than the white students.

The researchers found that, contrary to expectations, test scores were not statistically related to school poverty, neighborhood poverty, racial concentration, or even ranking of schools (except in the case of whites). They did find that African Americans, American Indians, and Hispanics were underrepresented in the top ranked schools. African Americans were 4.5 times as likely to be found in schools ranked low in math, and twice as likely to be found in schools ranked lowest in reading.

For both white students and students of color, success on the tests was positively correlated to how an individual had been tracked. Only 6.9 percent of students of color compared to 23 percent of white students had access to "gifted and talented" programs. This study suggests that tracking and the quality of the academic opportunities available in the school affects both the test score gap and the gap in academic performance generally. While these correlational studies are suggestive, they do not examine basic causes nor explain the pervasiveness and stability of the gap over prolonged periods of time.

Stereotype Vulnerability

A set of experimental studies conducted by Stanford University professor Claude Steele, an African-American psychologist, sought to explain the circumstances and situations that give rise to the race gap in test scores. He and colleagues gave equal numbers of African-American and white Stanford sophomores a 30-minute standardized test composed of some of the more challenging items from the advanced Graduate Record Examination in literature. Steele notes that all the students were highly successful students and test-takers since all Stanford students must earn SAT scores well above the national average in order to be admitted to the university.

The researchers told half the students that the test did not assess ability, but that the research was aimed at "understanding the psychological factors involved in solving verbal problems." The others were told that the test was a valid measure of academic ability and capacity. African-American students who were told that the test was a true measure of ability scored significantly lower than the white students. The other African-American students' scores were equal to the white students'. Whites performed the same in both situations.

The explanation Steele offers is that Black students know they are especially likely to be seen as having limited ability.

Groups not stereotyped in this way do not experience this extra intimidation. He suggests that "it is serious intimidation, implying as it does that if they should perform badly, they may not belong in walks of life where their tested abilities are important—walks of life in which they are heavily invested." He labels this phenomenon "stereotype vulnerability. . . ."

Signithia Fordham, an African-American anthropologist, studied a Washington, D.C. public high school and focused on how the "hidden" and explicit curriculum shapes student aspirations and achievements, and how students of differing cultural, racial, and social backgrounds respond to the schooling experience. Hers is a multifaceted, complex study, including interviews, participant observation, questionnaires, and field notes, gathered over a four-year period. She concludes that for African-American students, patterns of academic success and underachievement are a reflection of processes of resistance that enable them to maintain their humanness in the face of a stigmatized racial identity. She shows that African-American adolescents' profound ambivalence about the value and possibility of school success is manifest as both conformity and avoidance. Ambivalence is manifest in students' motivation and interest in schoolwork, which of course includes mastery of standardized test-taking skills. . . .

Standardized tests are a particularly insidious form of institutionalized racism. . . .

These three studies taken together suggest three related explanations for the race gap in academic achievement and in test scores. First, are students' perceptions of the opportunities in the wider society and the realities of "making it." Second, are the educational opportunities available in the educational system itself—within school districts, schools, and each classroom. Third, are the cumulative psychic and emotional effects of living in a social world saturated with racist ideology, and where racist practices and structures are pervasive and often go unnamed.

Gap in Test Scores

There has been long-standing concern over the race gap in test scores. What is almost always overlooked is the size and educational significance of the test score gap. Most people assume that the statistical gap in scores between persons of color and whites is enormous. It is not. Depending on the test the difference varies but hovers in the range of 10 percent. This difference in average scores has persisted over time, regardless of the type of test, whether it is an 'IQ' test, norm-referenced or proficiency test, regardless of a test's publisher, or regardless of the educational level of the test-taker, be it kindergarten or graduate school. . . .

Among the more commonly heard explanations for the gap in standardized test scores is that the tests themselves are culturally and racially biased. What this has usually been taken to mean is that the bias is lodged in the content or language of individual test items. In the early years of mental measurement, the racism of the test items was blatant. In more recent years, major test publishers have made efforts to review and eliminate items with overt cultural and racial bias. Though item bias remains, it is implausible to conclude that all the publishers in all their tests knowingly or unknowingly managed to create tests with an almost identical ratio of biased to unbiased items. The fact that scores on all commercially produced tests show the same 8–10 percent gap suggests that the gap cannot be fully explained by racial or cultural bias lodged in individual test items. Rather, the bias is *systemic and structural*—that is, built into in the basic assumptions and technology of standardized testing in the way the tests are constructed and administered, the way results are reported, and in the organizational structure and administrative rules of the accountability system itself.

Numerical Scales

There is perhaps no clearer illustration of how the differences among the races are greatly exaggerated and distorted than the numerical scales used to report results. There is, as I have noted, about a 10 percent difference in scores between white and nonwhite students. On a 100 point scale, this 10 percent difference constitutes a gap of ten points. However, California's Academic Performance Index or API (which is based entirely on students' scores on the Stanford 9 achievement Test) creates a 200 to 1000 point scale, and a 10 percent difference in scores morphs into a formidable 100 points. . . .

Standardized tests are a particularly invidious form of institutionalized racism because they lend the cloak of science to policies that have denied, and are continuing to deny, persons of color equal access to educational and job opportunities. An educational accountability system based on standardized testing—though predicated on "standardized" measurements which are purportedly neutral, objective, and color-blind—perpetuates and strengthens institutionalized racism.

Significant school reform is not possible without significant reform of the current system of national and state educational assessments. Change will come about only in response to pressure by coalitions and alliances that cut across political, social class, racial, and ideological lines.

We as a nation will continue to differ profoundly on how schools ought to educate, what an educated person ought to know, and on how students learn best. We must not allow governments, panels of corporate executives, and remote "experts" to impose a singular view of curriculum and learning.

5

Test Preparation Helps Students Learn

Jay Mathews

Jay Mathews is a writer for the Washington Post *and covers issues on education.*

The prevailing view that preparing students to score well on standardized tests, or "teaching to the test," has little or no educational value is distorted. Teaching students to excel on assessment exams does not involve endless drilling and memorization. Instead, while abiding by state standards, teachers create their own exams and instruct students how to score well on standardized tests by using critical thinking and analyzing skills. Consequently, discussions on teaching to the test would be more productive if they focused on which methods work best for students and their studying habits.

All signs point to 2006 being a crucial year for testing in America, with the first national results from the new SAT due, as well as significant changes underway in how states use the tests that rate schools under the No Child Left Behind law. If only, then, we could figure out a way to speak clearly to each other about what we think of the many tests our children are taking. Let's start by trying to clarify what I consider the most deceptive phrase in education today: "teaching to the test."

Teaching to the test, you may have heard, is bad, very bad. I got 59.2 million hits when I did a Google search for the phrase, and most of what I read was unfriendly. Teaching to the test made children sick, one article said. Others said it rendered test scores meaningless or had a dumbing effect on instruction. All of that confused me, since [over 20] years of visiting classrooms I have yet to see any teacher preparing kids for exams in ways that were not careful, sensible and likely to produce more learning.

There are, of course, ways to teach to the test that are bad for kids and that occur now and then in schools. Principals afraid that their scores would look bad have forced teachers to go over the same questions from old tests day after day, to prepare for some state assessment. But there is no evidence that this happens often. Strong teachers usually raise a ruckus, administrators back down and everybody goes back to the traditional lesson reviews that all good teachers use.

When we say "teaching to the test," we should acknowledge that we are usually not talking about those drill fests. Rather, we often use the phrase to refer to any course that prepares students for one of the annual state assessment exams required under the No Child Left Behind Act. For reasons that escape me, we never say a teacher is "teaching to the test" if she's using a test she wrote herself. We share the teacher's view that what she is doing is helping her students learn the material, not ace the test. But if she is preparing the class for an exam written by some outsider, the thinking goes, then she must be forced to adhere to someone else's views on teaching and thus is likely to present the material too quickly, too thinly, too prescriptively, too joylessly—add your own favorite unattractive adverb.

To Help Kids Learn

Yet if you asked the thousands of educators who have written the questions for the state tests that allegedly produce all these terrible classroom practices, they would tell you their objective is the same as the classroom teacher's: to help kids learn. And if you watched the best teachers at work, as I have many times, you would see them treating the state test as nothing more than another useful guide and motivator, with no significant change in the way they present their lessons.

Those who complain are not really talking about teaching to the state test. Unless teachers sneak into the counseling office and steal a copy, which can get them fired, they don't know what's on the test. They are teaching not to the test but to the state standards—a long list of things students are supposed to learn in each subject area, as approved by the state school board.

Hardly anybody complains about teaching to a standard. Teacher-turned-author Susan Ohanian is trying to change this, and she refers to all advocates of learning standards as "Standardistos." But she has not made much headway, mostly because standards make sense to parents like me. We are not usually included in discussions of testing policy, but we tend to vote in large numbers, and everybody knows that any governor or president who came out against standards for schools and learning would soon be looking for work in the private sector.

So why do we still talk about how terrible it is to teach to the test? I think it comes from our fear of the unknown. Those of us who are not teachers don't know what is going on in our children's classrooms. And teachers don't know what harm might come to them from the test results, as interpreted by often-wrongheaded people such as principals, superintendents, politicians and, particularly, parents.

Conversations about this would go more smoothly if we didn't have such distorted views of what teaching to the test means. We might instead turn the discussion to what methods of instruction work best or how much time our children should spend studying.

In some classes, such as the Advanced Placement, International Baccalaureate and Cambridge courses that have become popular in Washington area high schools, the need to prepare for a challenging exam outside of the teacher's control has often produced a remarkable new form of teamwork. Teacher and student work together to beat an exam that requires thought and analysis, not just memorization. If that is teaching to the test, let's have more of it.

6

Test Preparation Does Not Benefit Students

Steve Peha

Steve Peha is president and founder of Teaching That Makes Sense, Inc., an education consulting and reform organization based in North Carolina.

Rigorous assessment testing and academic standards have led to the rise of "teaching to the test" in classrooms, or extensively preparing students to succeed on assessment exams. However, the current teaching-to-the-test culture in the nation's schools does not prepare students for college or career success. In the United States, very few states have standards for technology, emotional intelligence, and financial literacy. Moreover, test preparation teaches students empty testing skills, rote memorization, less writing, and how to pass minimum competency tests, which many states are lowering. Unless state standards change, most students will graduate from high school unprepared for higher education and the workforce.

Over the last 17 years, every state in the country has gone through an arduous process of creating academic standards for their students. These standards represent the new curriculum. But is it really so new? Or have we merely codified the traditional academic values of the past? How do we know that the standards-based system we've created will get kids ready for college, improve workforce preparedness, and serve our society's needs in the future? For businesses looking to hire the workforce of the future, these are crucial questions.

The guiding principle of the standards movement is simple: what gets standardized gets tested, what gets tested gets taught. By adhering strictly to the standards-based approach, schools can address the issue of curricular inconsistency and, over time, provide students with a better education. At least that's the theory.

Missing in Action

When I first heard about the standards movement in the early 1990s, I was excited. What a great idea, I thought back then, to align our curriculum with current thinking on what kids needed to be successful in life. And even though I've never been a big fan of testing, I liked what politicians were saying about using testing to ensure a rigorous curriculum and establish high expectations.

[T]here remains . . . a profound gap between the knowledge and skills most students learn in school and the knowledge and skills they need in typical 21st century communities and workplaces.

But a comprehensive curriculum aligned to real-world requirements measured by rigorous testing isn't what we got. As a recent study by Achieve, Inc. called "The Expectations Gap: A 50-State Review of High School Graduation Requirements," concluded: "No state requires its graduates to take the courses that reflect the real-world demands of work and postsecondary education."

And this is hardly an isolated opinion. A report entitled "Crisis at the Core: Preparing All Students for College and Work," from ACT, Inc., the independent non-profit organization that publishes the popular ACT college admissions test, had this to say: "Far too many of the seniors in the class of 2004 . . . aren't ready for college or the workplace. And it seems unlikely that students already in the pipeline will be doing much better." In a similar vein, another report, "Learning for the 21st Century," published by The Partnership for 21st Century Skills, stated that even after more than a decade of work on standards-based reform "there remains ... a profound gap between the knowledge and skills most students learn in school and the knowledge and skills they need in typical 21st century communities and workplaces."

Instead of setting high standards, we seem to have lowered the bar to the point where students can pass tests by getting only 50%-60% of the points available. And while this problem could be fixed simply re-norming the scoring systems and raising the requirements for passing, our curriculum itself may have more fundamental weaknesses.

So if the current approach to standards and testing isn't addressing the skills students need to succeed at work ... perhaps the choices that were made originally need to be rethought.

Instead of focusing standards on the future, we seem to have focused them on the past. While most states have standards in traditional subject areas like reading, writing, math, social studies, and science, most students are not required to study these disciplines very deeply. In addition, few states have comprehensive standards for things like:

- Technology. While most kids do get some experience focused on basic computer operation, there's virtually nothing for kids in areas like computer programming, database development, interactive design, or information theory.

- Emotional Intelligence. Popularized by researchers like psychologist Daniel Goleman, emotional intelligence, or "EQ" as it is sometimes called, has been shown to be a significantly stronger predictor of career success than good grades or high scores on traditional achievement tests.

- Financial Literacy. Money management and "personal" economics are crucial disciplines everyone needs to master to some degree. They also come in handy in the world of work, not just for accountants and project managers, but for all employees who benefit from understanding the financial profile of their companies, industries, and professions.

Educators would tell us that the current curriculum is full to bursting, that there isn't even time to teach what is already required. And from my experience, they would be right. So if the current approach to standards and testing isn't addressing the skills students need to succeed at work, and if there's no room left in the school day to pack in the skills of career-readiness, perhaps the choices that were made originally need to be rethought. And perhaps business leaders need to be involved in the rethinking.

The Realities of Rationing and Rationalizing in a Test-Driven System

To get a sense of what our kids are really studying, it's helpful to look beyond state standards documents to the evolving structure of testing and the practical impact this is having on how schools decide where to put their time and energy. Instructional time is a finite resource and how that time is spent is increasingly determined by the way school funding is tied to test performance. Every teacher has to make hard choices every day on how much time to devote to which aspects of the curriculum. And these days, it only makes sense to spend time on what is tested.

The most powerful vector in the new calculus of curriculum planning is the Bush Administration's No Child Left Behind legislation. Currently, NCLB requires states to test children in grades 3–8 in math and reading, a requirement that will likely be extened into high school in the coming year. From the day-to-day perspective of principals and teachers, this means school resources will increasingly be directed to helping children in specific sub-groups meet minimum requirements in reading and math.

[F]rom 1998 to 2003, we made almost no progress at all (just a slight gain in math); some states even got worse in some subjects.

Time and money are finite resources in our schools, and even though it isn't always this way, a zero-sum psychology pervades education culture. The result is that resources spent in one area are resources lost in others. And as the consequences for poor performance become more concrete, resources are increasingly allocated based on test scores. This is exactly what the architects of the current accountability system intended, so in this sense, reform could be said to be working well. But unintended—though entirely predictable—consequences could negate meaningful gains in student learning and undermine legitimate progress.

Cause and Effect

Over the last 10 years that I have been working in schools across the country, the most noticeable effects of the standards movement that I have witnessed are:

- More teaching to the test, less teaching to the students. Today, teachers focus more on contrived activities, sample test items, timed pre-tests, and other test prep techniques as opposed to research-based best practice methods. Authenticity, meaning, and differentiation are considered less important despite an overwhelming research consensus that these are key elements of high quality instruction.

- More rote learning, less real learning. The popularity of scripted lessons and programmed scope-and-sequence instruction has risen dramatically. Kids fill out more worksheets, answer more questions at the end of textbook chapters, and participate in more drills. Critical thinking is increasingly confined to pre-planned publisher-supplied exercises that closely resemble problems on tests.

- More reading, less writing. NCLB requires no proficiency in writing. As a result, states have already begun cutting back on writing assessments to save money. At the same time, colleges and companies, faced with increasingly large numbers of poorly prepared students and employees, are increasing the amount of remedial writing training they provide.

- More minimum competence, less maximum achievement. State tests, which are used to calculate NCLB performance, are "pass-fail" minimum competency tests. And the percentage of points needed to pass is low—generally between 40% and 60%. Many states are actually in the process of lowering their requirements even further or exercising statistical loopholes in current legislation that would allow them to exempt more students from being counted.

In my experience, the standards movement has had the effect of encouraging schools to move from best practice to bad practice all in the name of raising scores. And scores have gone up. Sort of. Scores on state tests have risen appreciably in most subjects and at most grade levels. But scores on the National Assessment of Educational Progress tell a very different story. Why the discrepancy? Because you can't prep for it.

Only some schools take the NAEP and they don't know who they are until just before the test. There are no sample released items, no test prep booklets, and no pre-aligned curriculum from a publisher who also owns the company that wrote the test. It's a test teachers can't teach to. It's also a national test—the same for every kid who takes it. By contrast, the 50 different state tests vary widely in degree of difficulty. For these reasons, the NAEP provides a more accurate view of how we're doing. And according to these numbers we're not doing well: from 1998 to 2003, we made almost no progress at all (just a slight gain in math); some states even got worse in some subjects.

A Contradiction in Terms

As I read the research on workforce preparedness and talk to business people around the country, I notice another contradiction. While surveys of business leaders indicate overwhelming support for the current approach to standards-based reform, much of the same research shows that the skills students are developing in standards-driven schools are the not the skills the business community says it needs.

Perhaps it's too early to tell how this will shake out. Perhaps, as our political leaders contend, we just need to give it more time. But when I think about what I see in classrooms across the country, I'm disinclined to be that patient. Standing at the intersection of classroom and board room, I don't see how the current approach will deliver the results we need when it comes to workforce preparedness.

To have a workforce capable of helping businesses meet the challenge of an increasingly competitive global economy, a different approach to reform is needed—one that focuses on helping students develop high levels of proficiency in the real-world competencies they will need to succeed in the workplace of tomorrow.

Employers know best what that world is and how it is likely to change in the future. So it just makes sense for them to speak up and assert their values—and for educators and politicians to start listening. If current reform is based on standard transmission, business needs to kick it into overdrive.

7

High-Stakes Testing Improves Education

S. Paul Reville

S. Paul Reville is a lecturer on education at the Harvard University Graduate School of Education and executive director of the Pew Forum on Standards-Based Reform.

In January 2002, the No Child Left Behind Act (NCLB) was signed by President George W. Bush, furthering state and national standards in the classroom and school accountability. Under the NCLB, high-stakes testing—in which students take standardized state or national exams that have important consequences on placement decisions, teachers, schools, or districts—has gained major importance and consequently strengthened education and student performance. The State of Massachusetts serves as a prime example: After implementing statewide high-stakes testing reform in the early 1990s, student achievement on numerous accounts have soared. The failure to set high standards for students, regardless of background or race, is akin to discrimination.

In the early 1990s, a very ambitious school reform agenda emerged in Massachusetts as a result of the advocacy of the Massachusetts Business Alliance for Education (MBAE). In 1991, the MBAE presented its reform agenda, titled "Every Child a Winner!" to state policy makers. [Former] Gov. William Weld and legislative leaders embraced and refined the

S. Paul Reville, "High Standards Plus High Stakes Equals High Achievement in Massachusetts," *Phi Delta Kappan*, vol. 85, no. 8, April 2004, pp. 591–97. Reproduced by permission.

MBAE reform concept, ultimately shaping it into the Massachusetts Education Reform Act of 1993. This omnibus bill included the basic goals, assessment, and accountability elements of standards-based reform; a variety of system improvements, including charter schools; and a massive refinancing of education.

The Massachusetts reform strategy developed as a response to rising concerns among business and higher education leaders that the state's high school graduates were not well prepared to meet entry-level challenges in employment or college. In light of increased international competition, changes in the economy, a greater focus on equity, and the demands of an increasingly knowledge-based society, these leaders concluded that the public education system was not responding adequately to the challenges of the 21st century. The achievement bar had been raised, and consequently the importance and value of education to both individuals and society was rapidly increasing. The reformers' standards-based vision of a transformed, accountable system that could deliver equity and excellence was homegrown but informed by strategies being adopted in other states and at the federal level. It is noteworthy that the reformers' vision reflected an unusual national phenomenon—the convergence of business/economic and civil rights/equity interests around building a high-performance education system.

The Massachusetts Case

The Massachusetts standards-based reform strategy calls for high learning standards for all (and all means *all*) students, regular assessment to track progress for diagnostic and accountability purposes, and a set of consequences—that is, a performance-based accountability system for both educators and students. Equally important and too often forgotten, the strategy calls for both *capacity building*, providing teachers the training and support they need to assist students in meeting the new higher goals for education, and *opportunity to learn*, providing each student with high-quality teaching, a curriculum aligned with the standards, regular feedback on performance, and extra help when needed.

The Massachusetts standards were designed to reflect the requirements for success in higher education, employment, and citizenship. They state, in precise language, what children should know and be able to do at various stages of their education. While standards articulate expected results—a set of outcome indicators that are subject to measurement—they do not dictate a particular curriculum or form of instruction. Standards do not imply standardization; rather, they are goals that teachers, in their professional discretion, strive to achieve in varying ways.

In the end, standards-based reform is all about fairness.

A corollary of the high expectations for all students is the belief that fairness requires the state to have the same high expectations of all students, irrespective of their backgrounds. These reforms seek to realize the American myth, sadly so far from reality, that public schools are "the great equalizer." In pursuit of this goal, reformers refuse to continue to make the automatic assumption that we should have higher educational expectations for affluent children than we have for poor children. We know that a grade of A earned in a suburban school has usually represented far more learning than the typical A earned in an inner-city school. These reforms say that those discriminatory expectations are now intolerable. We believe not only that all children can learn at high levels but that the knowledge now exists to make this happen. All students are entitled to graduate from school having achieved proficiency— i.e., having mastered the knowledge and skills they will need to succeed in higher education, in future employment, as citizens, and as heads of families.

A Diagnostic Tool

The tests, an integral part of the reform strategy, are often confused with the overall reform. Tests are merely the yardstick with which progress is measured. In addition to being an instrument of accountability, tests are a diagnostic tool that can provide valuable information to teachers. Critics are fond of proclaiming the obvious—education cannot be improved by tests, and "no one ever fattened a cow by weighing it." Of course, no reformer ever thought so. The tests were instituted to measure the degree to which the educational goals were being realized, to gauge the degree to which students had attained proficiency, and to expose the weaknesses of current strategies and thereby force action for improvement.

Under the Massachusetts reforms, performance matters. Learning matters not only for the students but also for the adults in the education system. No longer is "trying hard" good enough. Incentives were introduced to focus students on learning and to focus policy makers, administrators, and teachers on establishing the conditions that will enable all students to attain the high standards. The nature of the education industry has been fundamentally and forever changed by this introduction of accountability for results.

In the end, standards-based reform is all about fairness. Fairness demands clear and challenging standards that reflect the knowledge and skills all students will need to succeed in this economy, in this democratic society, in a life of continuing learning, and as heads of families. Fairness demands that we expect all students to master the same challenging core skills and knowledge, even though many may achieve well beyond the core. Fairness means that we provide every student with the opportunity to learn and that we hold all of our students and those charged with educating them accountable for their respective shares of the learning process. Fairness requires us to award every student a diploma that actually stands for the achievement of a defined body of learning and not merely for "time served." Fairness requires that we discipline the system to deliver full learning opportunities for all children. Fairness means providing incentives for achievement; relevant data to all teachers, parents, and students; and help to those who need it. Fairness demands that we do not artificially shield students from stress and judgment by society, since this is the reality of the world they inhabit. Fairness demands consequences, not excuses, for performance.

On the 2000 National Assessment of Educational Progress (NEAP) science exam, 43% of Massachusetts' fourth-graders—the highest percentage in the nation—scored at or above the proficient level.

Implementation

Implementation of the reform began in the summer of 1993, and progress has been remarkably steady, thanks to the diligence of many educators and the continued support of several governors, an assortment of legislative leaders, the state board of education, and the business community. To be sure, there have been major controversies over curriculum frameworks, testing, stakes, charter schools, and other issues, but the basic architecture of the reform—higher standards and greater accountability in exchange for more resources for building capacity—has remained intact. Indeed, the Massachusetts strategy has been reinforced, however clumsily, by the heavy hand of the federal No Child Left Behind (NCLB) Act of 2001.

Massachusetts' standards, while difficult and time-consuming to develop, have been rated by organizations such as Achieve, Inc., as some of the best and highest in the nation. Likewise, the assessments, which include substantial open-ended portions, have earned the praise of such national groups as the Education Trust. The Massachusetts Comprehensive Assessment System (MCAS) is rigorous, publicly transparent, and well aligned with the state's Curriculum Frameworks. In the area of accountability, we have held the line on insisting that all students meet the high performance standards. We have done less well at holding districts, schools, and educators accountable for providing each student with an opportunity to learn. The possible adoption of "value-added" analysis and the pressure of NCLB are accelerating progress on system accountability. In the meantime, there is still much evidence that the indirect pressure of accountability has caused a variety of school improvements, especially in the target getting of academic services to underachieving students. . . .

Historically, tests without stakes or with very low stakes have seldom driven change or improvement.

While there is plenty of room for improvement and there are important gaps still to be closed, the current condition of education reform in Massachusetts is impressive. It is true that we cannot attribute all of our healthy indicators directly to the education reform, but, as reform has been the dominant feature of the last decade, the correlation appears to be strong. Here are a few examples of current national indicators of student achievement:

- On the 2000 National Assessment of Educational Progress (NAEP) science exam, 43% of Massachusetts' fourth-graders—the highest percentage in the nation—scored at or above the proficient level. In eighth grade, 42% scored at or above proficient, tied for second best in the nation.

- On the 2003 NAEP mathematics test, Massachusetts' fourth-graders tied for the highest score in the nation, with an average score of 242, significantly higher than the national average of 234. Eighth-graders tied for second in the nation, with an average score of 287. This score represented a five-point increase over the state's

2000 average and was 11 points higher than the national average of 276.

- On the 1998 NAEP writing exam, the state's eighth-graders shared second place with those from several other states. Massachusetts' eighth-graders scored an average of 155, while the national average was 148. And on the 2002 writing exam, eighth-graders scored 163, significantly higher than in 1998 and well above the national average of 152. . . .

The Case for High Stakes

Far and away the greatest and most divisive concern about education reform in Massachusetts has been the high stakes associated with MCAS. The stakes attached to the tests are a distinct policy intervention designed to create incentives to reward effort and performance. Although most of the controversy surrounding the standards movement revolves around the tests, the nub of the issue is really the stakes. The stakes make the test results matter, make performance count. The stakes are the fulcrum of the accountability system—an essential, pivotal component. The stakes create the urgency and give force to the push to dislodge the low expectations that characterize the status quo and result in the widely disparate impact of our current ineffective and unequal system of public schooling.

Historically, tests without stakes or with very low stakes have seldom driven change or improvement. For example, over the years in Massachusetts we have had countless standardized tests that have demonstrated the widespread, well-known, and commonly accepted inequity in education. Typically, the results of these tests were received with a shrug of resignation—but no changes. Now MCAS results demonstrate the same inequities, but, because there are stakes attached, suddenly change is everywhere. More resources and attention than ever before are directed toward those children whom we have historically underserved in education. Teachers are engaged in more professional development than ever before. Curriculum is changing to align with state standards. The results of a variety of assessments are available, are being widely used by educators, and are driving improvements in teaching. Everywhere, teaching strategies are being reconsidered and altered for greater effectiveness. In other words, meaningful stakes are the direct cause of substantial change in Massachusetts' schools.

Proponents of standards-based reform acknowledge the limits of tests and the cautions issued by virtually all testing experts and associations against making life-altering determinations on the basis of a single test. Reforms also believe that, before holding students responsible for their share of the learning, we should engage in the difficult work of holding adults accountable for having given the students the opportunity to learn. The strategy requires that educator accountability, with real stakes, needs to precede student accountability. However, none of these cautions dispels our belief that, as frequently argued by the late Al Shanker, the former president of the American Federation of Teachers, students must also have real consequences attached to their educational efforts.

[T]he results to date show that any kind of student, from any background or ethnicity, can achieve the standard if the learning conditions are right.

The question is how to administer the consequences fairly and appropriately. In Massachusetts, the state assesses students' progress at several intervals as they advance through the education system. There are no student stakes attached to MCAS performance until grade 10, when students must achieve a "competency determination" on MCAS in English and mathematics as a prerequisite for graduation. They must also meet all other local graduation requirements to receive a diploma. . . .

Critics claim that withholding a diploma for failure to achieve the competency standard on MCAS is a "punishment" to the student. Reformers believe that, although failure to graduate on time with one's class can be a painful inconvenience, it is a far greater injustice for educators to pass students on to college or employment knowing they lack the skills or knowledge that they will need to succeed. Instead of a punishment, we offer the benefit of additional education to all students—an education specifically aimed at providing them with the skills and knowledge they need to meet the next challenges in their lives. No one can guarantee a diploma in four years, but the state is now creating an entitlement for each student to attain competency, if not proficiency. That does not sound like a punishment to us.

The stakes here are high; no one should underestimate the severity of withholding a diploma. However, in an effort to build capacity, Massachusetts has more than doubled its financial commitment to eduction. In addition, the state's supreme court recently affirmed in *Student No. 9 and Others v. Board of Education and Others* that the state's accountability process is fair. We are making progress. Our goal of ensuring that all students meet the new higher standards is within reach. Most important, the results to date show that any kind of student, from any background or ethnicity, can achieve the standard if the learning conditions are right.

Spring of 2003—the last chance for the first graduating class whose members could be denied a diploma for failing the MCAS—was supposed to be the "train wreck." In fact, substantial numbers—thousands actually—representing virtually all subcategories of students, attained the standard. This outcome demonstrates that the standard is reasonable and well within the reach of all of our students. They are not prevented from attaining this standard by virtue of their DNA, their race, their social class, or their neighborhood. All students do it if we figure out how to assist each and every one. Here are the MCAS results to date:

- For the graduating class of 2003, 95% of all students have passed both exams and graduated; 92% of African American students have passed English, 90% have passed mathematics, and 88% have passed both. For Latinos, the numbers are 90%, 88%, and 85% respectively. For English-language learners, 86% passed English, 90% passed mathematics, and 83% passed both. And for disabled students, the numbers are 90%, 83%, and 85% respectively.

- Virtually every district in the state showed significant improvement on the 2001 MCAS exam, gains that were sustained in 2002. The improvement has been most dramatic at the high school level, where the percentage of students scoring at the proficient level or higher has risen from 24% to 44% in mathematics and from 38% to 59% in English since 1998. . . .

Time is no longer the constant in education. Learning is the constant, and time must vary to meet the educational needs of all students. The new educational promise is about mastery, not seat time. Social promotion clearly is not healthy for schools or students, nor is retention as conventionally practiced, with students literally repeating the same work at a particular grade level. However, more instructional time, different kinds of instruction, higher expectations, and more opportunities will work. In the end, helping to guide students to mastery, even if it takes more instructional time, is infinitely preferable to passing them on, unqualified, to certain failure. Misguided sympathy leads many to see it as generous to exempt students from the same kind of stakes in education that life routinely imposes on them. But students don't need waivers or exemptions or protection. They need an opportunity to learn.

The Soft Discrimination of Low Expectations

Standards-based reform, and the assessment and stakes that animate it, is a conspiracy against the pervasive soft discrimination of low expectations. That is why this reform is premised on the belief that all students can attain the high standards of proficiency. We have widespread evidence that this belief is true. The challenge ahead is to hold everyone in education responsible for providing the teaching and learning conditions that will enable all students to attain the standard.

We are distracted with our 'testing battle' and consequently are losing ground in the war to force our society to do better by our children, particularly the least fortunate.

We face strong opposition. There is a great temptation among many of those sympathetic to the plight of poor and minority youths to "shoot the messenger." They would deny the evidence of assessment, dispute the stakes, and avoid the real issue of the failure of our current education system to provide all of our children with what they need to be successful in life.

Poverty is a powerful and persistent obstacle to learning. Standards-based reformers acknowledge the injury of poverty, but they reject the temptation to give up on children by declaring "poverty as destiny." Instead, we embrace the strategies needed to make education truly matter in improving the prospects of those born into economic disadvantage. As a nation, we make a gigantic investment in schooling. We have an obligation to expect and to deliver results. We know that education has been the ladder out of poverty for many. Our challenge is to make that ladder work for everyone. Our goal must be to get the conditions of teaching and learning right for each and every student.

We know that, in the end, all reforms will be only as good as the quality of teaching they engender in the classroom. Some critics cite the existence of certain retrograde "drill and kill" practices as evidence that reform is not working. Reformers see countless instances of constructive practice coupled with unprecedented results. They view poor teaching practice as an argument for intensified professional development rather than for abandoning standards.

It is also true that the quality of teaching will not improve simply by articulating and mandating higher standards. The effort to develop the teaching capacity needed to meet the audacious demands of school reform—high standards for all students—will require more help for teachers than has heretofore been provided.

In Massachusetts and across the nation, we are far from having attained our ambitious goals, but we are making progress and learning as we go. Some critics would have us abandon ship because school reform strategies have not instantly achieved universal success or demonstrated perfection. Those of us who believe in these strategies see them as having already struck a mighty blow for the poor and disadvantaged. We want to build on the progress, rather than letting the perfect be the enemy of the good. All of us in the world of education need to recommit to the goal of "proficient for all" by shouldering our respective responsibilities and accepting our accountability for providing each child with the opportunity to become proficient. A return to the status quo ante—the manifestly failing system of education that preceded these reforms—simply unacceptable.

A Powerful Strategic Instrument

The Massachusetts evidence shows that high-stakes testing is a powerful strategic instrument, which, when properly employed as an element of standards-based school reform, can be a vital lever for achieving equity in American public education. I unabashedly join with William Taylor, one of our nation's most distinguished civil rights advocates, who has stated, "The standards movement could be the most important vehicle for the educational progress of minority and poor students since *Brown v. Board of Education*."

It is a shameful waste that so many potential allies in the quest to make schools serve all children better—so many of us who should be on the same side campaigning together for equity and excellence—are so deeply divided by the strategies of standards-based reform. The school reform community, the civil rights community, and children's advocates across the country are at loggerheads over the issues of standards, assessments, and stakes for performance. In our vigorous disagreement, not only have we lost an opportunity to benefit children, but we have also alienated one another and set back the cause in which we all believe. Because we believe deeply, we argue passionately. Our rhetoric soars, and most of us indulge in demeaning or even demonizing our opponents, thus feeding a growing sense of fracture and alienation among those who should be unified in their interests. In so doing, we are expending our political and intellectual capital. We are distracted with our "testing battle" and consequently are losing ground in the war to force our society to do better by our children, particularly the least fortunate. Rather than expending our energies debating the instruments of accountability, we should be waging an educational war, replete with an army of strategies for improvement, against that "tyranny" of low expectations. Only then will all our children have the opportunity to be proficient and prepared to succeed in life.

8

High-Stakes Testing Is Flawed

Dan French

Dan French is executive director of the Center for Collaborative Education in Boston.

The No Child Left Behind Act, enacted in 2002, resulted in the rise of high-stakes testing in American schools and may be renewed in 2007. High-stakes testing comprises standardized state or national exams taken by students that influence important placement, curriculum, funding, or administrative decisions for themselves, their teachers, their schools, or their districts. These tests, however, are seriously flawed and have especially deleterious consequences on students and their education. Standardized tests are biased, prone to scoring errors, and have led to increased dropout and grade retention rates among minorities, particularly African Americans and Latinos. Instead of achieving equity and excellence in the nation's educational system, it has worsened existing problems.

Recently, a former biologist, who is now a teacher intern in Alaska, wrote to his professor the following in an e-mail discussion about testing:

> We inadvertently ran a test at the hatchery while I was there.
> . . . One culturist sampled his fish every week to check growth rates and calculate the feed, while the other culturist just fed what the fish would eat. Guess what? After six weeks

Dan French. "A New Vision of Authentic Assessment to Overcome the Flaw in High-stakes Testing." *Middle School Journal,* vol. 35, no. 1, 2003, pp. 14–23. Reprinted with permission from the National Middle School Association.

the fish that were left undisturbed had almost twice the growth rate of the ones that were sampled constantly. Why? Stress levels [of the fish]. Our kids are no different. Stress was incredibly high during testing week at my high school . . . and noticeable for a while after in some of my classes.

The advent of the No Child Left Behind federal legislation has plunged us into an unprecedented era of high stakes testing, with the presumption that testing and more testing, coupled with the threat of not being promoted from grade to grade and of not graduating from high school, will be the engine that drives improvement in instruction and student achievement. Yet there are many inherent flaws to this approach, an approach that, under a mantle of equity and excellence, threatens to undermine the tenets of exemplary middle grades practice, and leave behind the very students that the legislation and testing movement purport to be helping.

We need to examine the industry claims of validity and reliability of high-stakes standardized tests, and question the very reasons our government and the education industry have embraced these tests.

The Two Faces of Standards

In a society like ours that is stratified by race and income, we must have standards of what all students should know and be able to do upon graduating from middle to high school, and from high school. The absence of standards virtually guarantees stratified resources and access to knowledge, based upon income, color of skin, and the community and neighborhood in which one lives. For example, two Massachusetts Department of Education studies, prior to the state enacting education reform legislation in 1993, found profound differences in the coursework of algebra and U.S. history courses in suburban, rural, and urban districts—suburban students were given more homework, had longer class periods, had greater access to educational materials, and received a more rigorous curriculum than urban and rural students enrolled in courses with the same title. . . . Standards form a tool to promote high quality curriculum and instruction for all.

Standards that promote equity are broad and streamlined in nature; they are designed to ensure that every student graduates with the habits of mind, skills, and knowledge to be a contributing member of a democratic society and world and to be prepared for a future productive life. Broad, streamlined middle grades standards promote relevant and rigorous instruction and curriculum that builds upon the principles of early adolescent development. These standards allow for locally determined assessments that require students to demonstrate mastery over essential knowledge through varied means, including portfolios, demonstrations, and exhibitions.

However, standards can also reinforce and amplify the current inequities that pervade public education. It is with this understanding that the National Forum to Accelerate Middle-Grades Reform recently released the following statement on high stakes testing:

> The National Forum believes in standards and assessments that lead to high expectations, foster high quality instruction, and support higher levels of learning for every student. At the same time, the National Forum believes that no single test should ever be the sole determinant of a young adolescent's academic future, whether it be promotion to the next grade, special placement, or transition from the middle grades to high school.

With this lens, we need to take a careful look at the impact of linking state-level high stakes testing to the standards movement, and the resulting impact on curriculum and instruction. Ultimately, we need to examine its effects on student achievement, particularly those students that federal and state governments claim the standards and testing movement is most designed to help—low-income students and Black and Latino students. We need to examine the industry claims of validity and reliability of high stakes standardized tests, and question the very reasons our government and the education industry have embraced these tests. Finally, we need to ask ourselves if there is another way to employ standards as an equity tool that leads to more effective middle grades practice and that better assists every student to achieve at high levels.

No One Measure Can Do Justice

[Former *New York Times* education columnist Richard] Rothstein used a baseball example to question the veracity of using a single high stakes test to measure a student's knowledge:

> Mike Piazza, batting .332, could win this year's Most Valuable Player award. He has been good every year, with a .330 career batting average, . . . and a member of each All Star team since his rookie season. The Mets reward Piazza for this high achievement, at the rate of $13 million a year.
>
> But what if the team decided to pay him based not on overall performance but on how he hit during one arbitrarily chosen week? How well do one week's at-bats describe the ability of a true .330 hitter?
>
> Not very. Last week Piazza batted only .200. But in the second week of August he batted .538. If you picked a random week this season, you would have only a 7-in-10 chance of choosing one in which he hit .250 or higher.

Rothstein questioned the validity of assessing a student's knowledge at one point in time. Studies have documented that how students fare on standardized tests can be greatly influenced by a host of external factors, including stress over taking the test, amount of sleep, distractions at the testing site, time of day, emotional state, and others. Indeed, these influences most dramatically affect low-income students and students of color. [Psychologist Claude] Steele has found that

African-American students perform significantly below their potential on tests in which they know they are being assessed on their intellectual performance, largely due to what he calls "stereotype threats," a historical and well supported fear that tests created by the dominant culture will judge them to be wanting. We only need revisit the origins of testing in the United States—that of the eugenics movement and the rise in immigration in the early 1900s, resulting in IQ and Stanford-Binet tests as a means to sort and track students primarily based on race and income—to understand that the roots of high stakes testing lie in sorting students.

Standardized tests are also poor predictors of how well students can apply the knowledge that they do demonstrate on these tests. A recent study examined data from 18 states that have implemented high stakes testing programs to assess whether students gained any knowledge that they could apply elsewhere, other than learning the necessary facts for performing on a state's high stakes test. . . .

The number of test errors by the major testing companies are too numerous to detail. . . .

[Researchers Thomas] Kane and [Douglas] Staiger's 2001 research study found that "between 50 percent and 80 percent of the improvement in a school's average test scores from one year to the next was temporary and was caused by fluctuations that had nothing to do with long-term changes in learning or productivity". According to Kane and Staiger, these findings are caused by the variations in student population in a given grade from year to year, variations in test conditions, and the presence of rewards and punishments from the state or district. Other studies have concluded that students "lost" from the testing pool—through grade retention, dropping out, or being excluded from taking the test because of having special education or bilingual status—create the appearance of an improving school when in fact the opposite may very well be true.

Most importantly, standardized test scores are far from an accurate predictor of how students will do in later life, even as they take on the draconian role of determining a student's future life opportunities in many of our states. As former Harvard and Princeton presidents Derek Bok and William Bowen attest in their book *The Shape of the River*:

> [They] researched what became of 700 African-American students who would have been bumped out of their chosen schools [based solely] on test scores. About 70 of the freshmen became doctors, about 60 became lawyers, about 125 became business executives, more than 225 earned professional degrees or doctorates, more than 300 are leaders of civic activities. The average [annual] earnings of the 700 are more than $71,000. "Taken together, grades and scores predict only 15 to 20 percent of the variance among all students in academic performance and a smaller percentage among black students."

Are These Tests Even Reliable?

The high error rate that has been experienced in virtually every major testing program and state in the nation in which high stakes tests are used calls to question the validity of such tests. The number of test errors by the major testing companies are too numerous to detail, with many having disastrous effects on the students they are measuring. Some highlights include:

1. A Massachusetts history teacher found an error in one multiple choice question on the state's 8⁰ grade high stakes test which resulted in 666 students failing the test who would have otherwise passed, many of whom were retained in grade as a result.

2. In Minnesota in 2000, the testing company, NCS Pear-

son, made a scoring error on the tests of 47,000 students; of these, almost 8,000 eighth through twelfth grade students incorrectly received failing grades, with 54 high school seniors being denied diplomas until the scoring error was discovered.

3. In New York City in 1999 nearly 9,000 middle and high school students were mistakenly required to attend summer school because of test scoring errors by [California Testing Bureau] CTB/McGraw-Hill. McGraw-Hill admitted that they also made scoring errors in Indiana, Nevada, Tennessee, South Carolina, and Wisconsin.

4. In November 1998, Harcourt Brace misclassified as "below basic" or "basic" elementary students who had actually scored at "proficient" or "advanced" levels. The mistake was detected by a principal.

High error rates and poor reliability are some of the reasons why a multitude of respected national education organizations, including the National Forum for Accelerating Middle-Grades Reform and the American Educational Research Association, have issued public statements decrying the use of a single high stakes test to determine students' futures.

[T]he high stakes testing movement impedes the drive toward creating more academically challenging courses of study for middle grades students. . . .

The Hidden Consequences of High-Stakes Testing

While proponents of high stakes tests declare that their approach has led to increased gains in student achievement, and even narrowed the achievement gap by race and income, this is hardly the case. On the contrary, the students who are most negatively affected by the consequences of high stakes tests are low-income, Black and Latino. Massachusetts and Texas, leaders in the high stakes testing movement and widely bally-hooed as exemplary systems, are good cases to examine.

In Massachusetts, since the advent of their high stakes test, the Massachusetts Comprehensive Assessment System (MCAS), the percent of middle grades dropouts has increased. These dropouts are increasingly African American and Latino, 19 times and 14 times, respectively, more likely to drop out than their White peers. These students, who must be 16 in order to legally drop out, are the likely products of multiple years of being retained in grade. Grade retention, a critical correlate to dropping out of school, is on the rise and at all-time highs in many urban districts, as these districts strive to prevent students from entering grades with high stakes tests until they are deemed ready to pass. The number of students who are unaccounted for within each year's cohort of students as they pass from grade to grade has doubled. Most of these students have probably been held back in grade. . . .

In a 2001 Public Agenda Poll, 75% of parents and 90% of teachers felt that it is "wrong to use the results of just one test to decide whether a student gets promoted or graduates."

Narrowing the Window

This maze of high stakes tests invariably has its impact on where it matters most—the classroom and the relationship between teachers and students. In many states in the middle grades, we have witnessed a narrowing of the curriculum and a movement away from the type of curriculum and instruction that best assists middle grades students to learn and become productive citizens in our larger world. Studies have found that high stakes testing decreases choice in the classroom, decreases motivation to learn, focuses the curriculum on coverage at the expense of depth and understanding, and narrows the scope of instruction to more teacher-centered strategies rather than student-engaged instruction.

In fact, the high stakes testing movement impedes the drive toward creating more academically challenging courses of study for middle grades students and inhibits the creation of collaborative faculty teams of teachers engaged in discourse on improving instruction. In Massachusetts, which administers a high stakes test, all schools are required to develop individual student plans for any student that fails the math or English portion of the exam. Unfortunately, in some schools that have high percentages of low-income students, students of color, and students whose first language is other than English, upwards of 80% of students fall into this category. The result is that tremendous amounts of team common planning time are spent writing individual student plans, that end up looking the same, taking away valuable time from teachers' discussions of how to improve instruction through practices such as looking at student work, peer observation, data-based inquiry, and action research. . . .

Is This What the Public Wants?

If high stakes testing is having deleterious effects on the middle grades, why are we so passionately rushing down this path? Whose agenda is it? Do we really believe that highly prescriptive standards and high stakes testing present the ultimate solution to the complex and messy challenge of educating our increasingly diverse early adolescents?

This agenda is certainly not being driven by teachers and parents, those who best know what it takes to effectively educate our younger generation. An August 2000 Gallup Poll produced for *Phi Delta Kappan* found that only 13% of the public believed that a single standardized test was the best way to measure academic achievement, while 85% felt that the best way was either a combination of standardized and teacher-designed tests or portfolios of student's work and other demonstrations of academic competence. In a 2001 Public Agenda poll, 75% of parents and 90% of teachers felt that it is "wrong to use the results of just one test to decide whether a student gets promoted or graduates." In this same poll, 83% of teachers feared that "teachers will end up teaching to the tests instead of making sure real learning takes place," and 82% felt that "schools today place far too much emphasis on standardized tests".

A single score on a test should never stand as the sole measure of a student's knowledge, understandings, performance, and intellectual habits. . . .

What we have, then, is a high stakes testing movement being fueled, not by those who best know and care about the students in our middle schools, but by others outside of our public schools who have varied interests at heart. In 1999, NCS Pearson, a large testing company, reported more than $620 million in revenues, up 30% from the previous year. McGraw-Hill, another large testing company, also owns programs such as Open Court and Reading Mastery, two direct instruction programs that are being purchased in large numbers by districts striving to drive up their standardized test scores. State spending on testing has increased multifold. It is estimated that the K-12 standardized testing industry is as much as $1.5 billion per year. Business leaders and legislators have lined up behind this industry as a quick fix to the dilemmas of educating a diverse student population.

Summing Up the Damage

Excellent middle schools have as their foundation the following four strengths: rigor, relevance, relationships, and resources:

1. Rigor, or academic challenge which is personalized, that builds upon the relationships and experiences of young adolescents, and that prepares students to be literate,

participating members of a democratic society;

2. Relevance, in that the curriculum, instruction, and assessment has meaning, is developmentally responsive, and makes connections to students' lives and the world around them;

3. Relationships, in which middle schools are small and personalized enough so that every student is known well by at least one caring, nurturing adult in the school, and in which positive student relationships are fostered and valued within the classroom (in fact, [researcher Anthony] Bryk and [Barbara] Schneider suggest a correlation between strong, positive relationship and high trust levels with students' academic improvement); and

4. Resources, in which middle schools have maximum, charter-like control over budget, staffing, curriculum, governance, and time to best meet the needs of their unique student population, and, in the words of the National Forum to Accelerate Middle-Grades Reform, are used "to work to overcome systemic variation in resources and outcomes related to race, class, gender, and [achievement]."

Unfortunately, the high stakes testing movement has latched onto only one of these four criteria—rigor. Absent the other three criteria for excellent middle schools, high stakes testing ends up adopting the very narrow definition of rigor outlined in The American Heritage Dictionary: "Strictness or severity . . .; a harsh or trying circumstance . . .; a harsh or cruel act". Such conditions inevitably end up harming those students and schools who are most vulnerable.

Ultimately, state-level high stakes testing is a fundamentally flawed concept, and does not achieve the stated ends of equity and excellence. The current standardized testing movement undermines the vision of creating excellent and equitable middle grades schools that are academically challenging, developmentally responsive, and socially equitable by creating a narrow and rigid view of learning and teaching that exacerbates the inequities of our educational system and larger society. A single score on a test should never stand as the sole measure of a student's knowledge, understandings, performance, and intellectual habits, and should never be used to determine a student's future.

9

Standardized Testing Measures College Success

Jeffrey Penn

Jeffrey Penn is a reporter for the New York Academy of Sciences, a nonprofit, membership-based organization for the advancement of science, technology, and medicine.

The limitations and value of the SAT are intensely debated, but the standardized college admissions test continues to be a reliable predictor of college success. In addition, for some subjects, SAT scores are statistically more consistent predictors of college freshman grades than high school grades. The new version of the SAT, renamed the SAT Reasoning Test, was introduced in March 2005 and contains an essay section that measures writing abilities. Optimally, both high school grades and SAT scores are considered in admissions decisions, but the SAT remains an important assessment of cognitive abilities.

Despite some limitations and the intense criticism by opponents of standardized testing, colleges and universities can reliably use admissions tests to screen applicants, according to an expert who spoke on the subject during a November 19 [2001] lecture entitled "Predicting College Success Value and Limitations of the SAT, High School Grades and Other Factors" "The SAT is the most vigorously and well-researched test in the world, and yet nothing seems to be more controversial than the SAT," said Wayne Camara, vice president for development and Research at the College Board [the organization that administers the SAT].

Jeffrey Penn, "Expert Says SAT is Reliable Predictor of College Success, New SAT Will Measure Writing Ability," *The New York Academy of Sciences,* www.nyas.org. Reproduced by permission.

"Thousands of validity studies and intense analysis of the SAT reveals that it has helped to reliably predict college success when SAT scores are compared with college freshman grade point averages," Camara said. "And although there are fewer validity studies that explore overall success in college, the SAT is also a good indicator of four-year grade point averages," he added.

Admission Test Scores Are Reliable Predictor

According to Camara, the validity studies have consistently shown that high school grades are statistically the most reliable predictor of future academic success measured in college grade point averages, but that SAT scores are only slightly less able to predict success than high school grades. However, the combination of both grades and test scores is the most statistically reliable predictor.

"The SAT is actually a slightly better predictor than high school grades for projecting college freshman grades in specific subjects, particularly for individual math, science, and social science courses," Camara noted. And, Camara noted that high school grades over-predict college grades for Hispanic and African American males, and under-predict performance for females. "SAT scores are slightly better than high school grades at predicting female performance in college," he said.

"The SAT is designed to measure cognitive abilities needed to succeed in college, but of course it doesn't predict more subjective things like perseverance and good study habits necessary for succeeding in college," Camara pointed out "At the point of making decisions, admission directors must use the best information available, and admissions tests continue to be a valuable and reliable tool."

Competitive Environment and Misconceptions

Camara suggested that a more competitive admission environment has contributed to the scrutiny of the SAT. In addition, he said that there is a misconception among some students and parents that the SAT is the most important factor in the process.

"The College Board has been conducting an annual survey of college admissions directors for more than two decades," Camara said. Across the years, both four-year public and private institutions have consistently reported that high school grades are the most important factor in admission decisions and have always ranked it higher than scores from admission tests.

According to Camara, the survey has shown a slight increase in the importance of admission tests at public institutions, which he said might reveal that admission directors are using the test scores as a corrective to grade inflation. He also rejected what he said were misleading claims by anti-testing groups that a growing number of colleges are dropping the SAT in their admission procedures.

"Among four-year public institutions in the United States, 96 percent require an admission test today compared to 91 percent in 1979 and among four-year private institutions, 92 percent required admission tests, compared to 91 percent in 1979," Camara reported. Approximately 3.2 million SAT I and SAT II tests were administered in academic year 2001–2.

Does Coaching Work?

Camara suggested that the competitive environment has also contributed to the growing test-preparation and coaching companies, many of which make what Camara said was "inflated" claims for score gains on the test. According to College Board research, coaching has a consistent but very moderate impact on score gains in studies using a control group, leading to 25–35 point gains for commercial coaching companies.

"These 25–35 point gains are significantly lower than the 200-point gains that the coaching companies claim," Camara pointed out, "but many parents seem willing to continue spending money in order to buy their children any possible advantage."

Yet Camara advised parents to spend their resources and time encouraging their children to apply themselves in their high school studies and homework, rather than on banking on the promises of coaching companies.

New SAT To Include Writing Section

Whatever strategies parents and students employ, Camara said that there would continue to be a need for reliable predictors in the college admission process. After all, there is no reason to admit students who cannot succeed in college, only to drop out later with student loans to repay. Currently one-third of all students do not persist to the sophomore year, and one-half don't graduate within six years, Camara said.

In an effort to provide improved information to admission directors, the College Board will administer a new SAT beginning in March 2005. According to Camara, "the design objectives will maintain the value and quality of the new SAT so that it measures reasoning and critical thinking skills, reflecting curriculum, classroom practices and college skills."

"The new SAT will maintain or improve validity for predicting college success, maintain psychometric quality and maintain trend data, and ensure that changes will not exacerbate group differences," Camara said The new test will report three scores on a 200–800 scale, on sections that measure critical reading, math reasoning, and writing.

"The math section will be more curriculum-related and will retain open-ended items," Camara said. "but the quantitative comparison items will be removed. The critical reading section will contain more passages based on high school curriculum and the former section of analogies will be dropped."

The new writing section will include some multiple-choice items and a 25-minute essay that will be scored and digitally posted on the College Board's Web site, so that admission directors will have access to the essay.

10

Standardized Testing Does Not Measure College Success

Theodore A. O'Neill

Theodore A. O'Neill is dean of college admissions at the University of Chicago.

Standardized testing does not accurately predict college success or happiness. On the contrary, SAT scores are not objective and correlate to family income. However, such measurements are taken into primary consideration because it eases the process of admissions decisions; but training students to score well on standardized tests, measuring these scores, and using them for the task of selection comes at the cost of educating and evaluating students as complete candidates. Taking the easy way out and relying on test scores excludes historically marginalized students from pursuing higher education, such as those who are poor and speak English as a second language.

A recent article in *The New York Times* revealed some surprising news: The new SAT-I writing component, to be administered for the first time in March [2005] has inspired a return to handwriting lessons. The 25-minute writing portion of the test will be handwritten, and it will, after all, have to be read by graders, not machines. Scores may well be influenced, or even determined, by legibility.

Will students who do not get instruction in handwriting suffer? Will boys write less legibly than girls, and be judged less talented? Even more troubling, I wonder, will students from schools with the most resources have an advantage on such an examination?

I don't really wonder, of course, because we have been through all this before. Perhaps adding the writing section to the SAT will, as promised, lead schools to teach more writing (what kind of writing, whose version of good writing, remains to be seen)—and better penmanship. But what if the writing section hurts poor kids and first-generation English speakers? What if, as many of us predict, the writing portion is even more coachable than the other sections? (A college-counselor friend tells me that she knows a coach who can almost invariably bring a student to an 800 on the SAT writing test. He charges a lot.) What I do wonder is how will admissions officers, politicians, schools, families, and children deal with yet another examination that pretends to tell us something about—*what?*

As all school boards in America know, scores are the most easily manipulable measures of anything that might suggest quality in education.

When pressed, we admissions people say that the SAT scores add a bit of power, when considered alongside high-school performance, to our ability to predict first-year college grade-point averages. Do we ultimately care about first-year GPA's? We really want to be able to make the best estimate of who will ultimately be happiest and most successful in the particular educational setting our college provides. Test scores do not predict such happiness and success; so why do so many of us require the scores?

Making the Task of Selection Easier

The simple bad reason is that standardized-test results make the task of selection easier, because they offer the illusion of precision when assessing qualities that we say we value but cannot actually name. As all school boards in America know, scores are the most easily manipulable measures of anything that might suggest quality in education. Having the power to control what stands for quality, to train for scores, to select for scores, is so much easier than really educating, or than considering a whole candidate. No one really believes anymore that the scores are "objective," the one element in a college application that is comparable across applicants, schools, and states. Even the College Board, which administers the SAT, gave up that argument years ago when finally conceding that coaching can affect results. We would rather not admit, and the College Board would rather not tell us, that scores, in the aggregate, correspond to income of parents.

We who work in college admissions do what we do because we believe in the power of education to transform young lives and society. The vast majority of admissions counselors emphatically believe that students from groups historically excluded from higher education should be included, for the benefit of the students and the nation, and most certainly for the enhancement of the education offered at our institutions. What happens when we, the good guys, accede to the incessant testing, sorting, and labeling of students?

What will happen when we see that poor students, first-generation college students, and students for whom English is a second language do even less well on the new SAT than on the old? We will, of course, ignore the scores when it is appropriate to do so. Because of the relentless pressure from testing agencies and various powerful constituencies, we cooperate in requiring more testing. (The most selective colleges in the country want not only results from the tripartite SAT-I reasoning test but, in addition, results from three more SAT-II subject tests, with a lurking desire for results from five SAT-II tests—talk about redundancy in the name of higher selectivity!) Then we must disregard the very tests we require in order to do our work thoughtfully and fairly.

How long will legislatures and courts permit our willingness to ignore test scores that the world believes to be powerful, precise, and objective? If we adhere to the tests, we agree to punish poor kids. If we disregard the tests, we are at risk of being considered capricious, or irresponsible social engineers.

Time and Skill

Admissions officers could, of course, ask students to write for the college application rather than for the SAT, could pose questions interesting enough to capture the attention of smart kids and then read the responses with care and sensitivity—but that takes time and skill. We could sit and talk to students about their thoughts, reading, lives, dreams, and whatever else they feel is important to an understanding of who they are, but that takes time and skill. Schoolteachers could teach and evaluate without relying on Advanced Placement examinations and SAT-II's to direct their teaching and validate their successes, but that would take time and skill.

Even if the skill is available—a lot of skillful and devoted people work as teachers and admissions counselors—the time so frequently is not. Colleges all want more applications to move up in the rankings, and it's not just the big public universities that are swamped with admissions files to be read, usually by staffs that haven't grown as applications have increased. At the same time, the College Board is more and more insistent about selling its services, which we need to survive in the marketplace as it is now constructed, and which students are forced (by us) to use.

So, to our peril, we take the easy way out. Penmanship may improve at a lucky few schools; but what is lost as we stack the deck, once more, to the disadvantage of the least advantaged? What do we all lose when we pretend to make complicated and crucially important issues simple?

11

The New SAT Is
an Improved Test

John W. Harper

John W. Harper is an admissions counselor and a tutor in New York City.

Administered since 1926 in the United States, the SAT was significantly revised in March 2005. The changes were implemented by the College Board, the producer of the admissions exam, after the University of California system alleged that its scores were not a reliable predictor of college performance and reflected bias against minority students. The new SAT, or the SAT Reasoning Test, is straightforward, unbiased, raises standards, and fosters fair competition. The increased emphasis on writing ability and algebra ensures that SAT scores accurately assess reading, writing, and math skills and forecast the potential to succeed in college.

In late June [2002], the trustees of the College Board voted unanimous approval for the most dramatic changes in the history of the SAT, the venerable admissions test that is a gatekeeper of so many American colleges. Beginning in March 2005, the analogy questions that have tormented test-takers since the first SAT in 1926 (untruthful is to mendacious as circumspect is to cautious, etc.) will be abolished. In their place will be more reading comprehension questions, similar

John W. Harper, "The New, Improved SAT: Surprisingly the Revised College Admissions Test Is Better Than the Old One," *Weekly Standard*, vol. 7, no. 47, August 26, 2002.

to those that already make up most of the verbal test. The math section, which now tests arithmetic, geometry, and basic algebra, will add problems from advanced algebra, while the quantitative comparison questions (which is greater, 2x or x squared, etc.) will be dropped. Finally, a new, separately scored 50 or 60 minute writing test will be added, consisting of multiple choice questions on grammar and usage and a handwritten essay.

The immediate impetus for redesigning the SAT was the attack on the test launched early in 2001 by University of California president Richard Atkinson. Himself a cognitive psychologist and an authority on testing, Atkinson charged that the use of the exam was distorting educational priorities and practices. The SAT, he suggested, though intended to measure verbal and mathematical reasoning ability or aptitude independent of particular courses of study, in reality was more a measure of students' test-taking skills. Recounting a visit to his grandchildren's private school where he found 12-year-olds already being drilled weekly on SAT-type analogies, Atkinson argued that students were wasting valuable time inside and outside the classroom preparing for the test, time that could be better spent learning history or geometry or English.

[T]he SAT seems to be safe for the foreseeable future.

The End of the "Big Test"?

Atkinson also asserted that analysis of three decades of undergraduate data at the University of California had shown that the SAT II subject tests, in conjunction with high school grades, were actually a slightly better predictor of success in college than the SAT, and that adding the SAT to the mix improved the predictive power by only a trivial increment. (Interestingly, the same data also seem to show that the SAT II writing test is the best single predictor overall.) Since the SAT

II tests could thus be substituted for the SAT without any sacrifice of predictive validity, Atkinson recommended that the University of California system drop the SAT requirement in favor of the SAT II or similar achievement tests assessing mastery of specific college-preparatory subject matter.

Atkinson's bombshell was front-page news. Losing the University of California as a customer would have been a severe setback for the authority and predominance of the SAT— perhaps a fatal one. Indeed, several liberal opponents of standardized testing gleefully predicted that California's defection would prove to be the beginning of the end for the "Big Test." To many conservatives, on the other hand, Atkinson was not a hero but a villain. They suspected him of attempting an end run around Proposition 209, which had banned racial preferences in California's public colleges and universities.

How this new test, therefore, could be of use to anyone who seeks to weaken standards for the sake of racial preferences or "diversity" is hard to see.

On this view, liberal egalitarians were bent on killing the test because it stood in the way of achieving a politically correct ethnic mix on campuses; the attack on the SAT was the vanguard of an attack on all standards of merit. In truth, some of Atkinson's statements lent support to these suspicions. He did argue that the SAT was unfair or perceived as unfair to minorities and that it devastated the self-esteem of otherwise accomplished people; and he did plead in the long run for a less test-driven, "more holistic, more comprehensive" evaluation of candidates. (And, independent of the SAT controversy, recent University of California admissions preferences for those who have suffered various hardships or "life challenges" strike some critics as so selectively awarded as to constitute backdoor affirmative action.) But in hindsight it is clear that both liberal and conservative responses to Atkinson tended to fixate on the issue of abolishing the SAT, while ignoring his central demand: to replace aptitude tests with tests of achievement.

An Out-and-Out Achievement Test

Though the College Board initially reacted to Atkinson's attack with incredulity—president Gaston Caperton sputtered that dropping the SAT from college admissions would be like dropping grades—after reflection, the test-makers settled on a shrewder strategy of reforming the exam in order to preserve it. While it has never really been a pure test of aptitude or native intelligence independent of prior schooling (if a student has not learned basic algebra and geometry, no amount of aptitude will get him through the math), the SAT is nevertheless a direct descendant of early twentieth-century IQ tests, and has long been at pains to distinguish itself from its controversial ancestor. A gradual shift away from characterizing the exam as a test of intelligence or aptitude has been evident for many years. As the author David Owen has observed, "intelligence" has been a "dirty word" among the test-writers, "IQ" an "obscenity"; and in recent years, "aptitude has become almost as unmentionable as IQ."

Accordingly, the name "Scholastic Aptitude Test" was officially discarded in 1993, and the College Board now weirdly insists that "SAT is not an initialism; it does not stand for anything." (Likewise, the deliberately uninformative terms "SAT I" and "SAT II" now obfuscate a once clear distinction between tests of aptitude and tests of achievement.) Bringing this trend to a culmination, the College Board has essentially met Atkinson's challenge by recasting the SAT as an out-and-out achievement test of college preparatory reading, writing, and math. Since Atkinson now says he is "delighted" with the College Board's reforms, the SAT seems to be safe for the foreseeable future.

And the new SAT will be a better test than the current one, in several respects. Most important, it does not lower standards, it raises them. With the addition of a writing test and problems from second-year algebra, students will have to know more and do more. The new test will even last half an hour longer than the current three hours. How this new test, therefore, could be of use to anyone who seeks to weaken standards for the sake of racial preferences or "diversity" is hard to see.

Making the SAT a straightforward test of achievement . . . will send an unmistakable message about what is most important to colleges.

Despite what Atkinson and other critics often charge, the current SAT is not racially biased, even though "underrepresented" (i.e. non-Asian) minorities do receive significantly lower average scores. But since the point of the SAT is to predict success in college, lower scores would constitute bias only if the test predicted poorer college grades than these minorities actually receive. In fact, as William G. Bowen and Derek Bok (proponents of both affirmative action and standardized testing) observe in their 1998 book, "far from being biased against minority students, standardized admissions tests consistently predict higher levels of academic performance than most blacks actually achieve." (Though seldom acknowledged in public debate, this "overprediction mystery" is familiar to psychometricians; the other side of the coin is that the SAT underpredicts the college performance of most Asians.) At any rate, given the racial sensitivities involved, not the least of the new curriculum-based test's advantages will be that it is unequivocally not a test of IQ or innate ability. If under the new exam minority scores continue to lag, it will be obvious that the reason is not that the SAT is a racially biased intelligence test but that the public schools are simply failing to give minority students the skills necessary for success in college.

Clearly Superior

As Atkinson's argument implies, at least two issues must be considered in the choice of a college admissions test. First, what kind of students does the test choose? And second, how does the test shape the education of those who take it? If it is inevitable that students will try to prepare for the test and that high schools will try to teach to it, the second question is no less important than the first. And here the new SAT is clearly superior.

If what is tested inevitably becomes what is taught, far better to have an admissions exam that reinforces the curriculum rather than undermines it or distracts from it. The [former] SAT diverts students' time and attention away from real learning to analogy drills, memorization of vocabulary, and sterile test-taking skills. It also devalues the high school curriculum, given the paramount importance that students and parents rightly suspect colleges place on the SAT. (Former Dartmouth assistant director of admissions Michelle Hernandez reports in her 1997 book that, contrary to the official line of virtually everyone, admissions committees are much more impressed by high SAT scores than by all A's on a high school transcript. "It used to surprise me that even the Director of Admissions would make excuses for students with extremely high scores [and B grades]. . . . 'With those scores I bet Caroline was just bored with her classes and her teachers. . . .' You would never hear the same argument for someone with a number-one rank and all low 500 scores. . . . I cannot overstate the importance of standardized testing, despite what admissions officers might tell you.")

Making the SAT a straightforward test of achievement in reading, writing, and math will send an unmistakable message about what is most important to colleges. Of course, the [former] SAT II tests already measure achievement (as do the advanced placement exams), but since only the most selective colleges require them, the great majority of students never take them. If the goal is to alter the incentives confronting all college-bound students, there is no better way than by reforming the SAT.

Sifting Out "Diamonds in the Rough"

As for the other issue raised by the choice of admissions test—what kind of students are selected—one must ask: Even if the new test will be as good as or better than the old one at predicting success in college, will nothing valuable be lost in the break with aptitude testing? The classic rationale for an admissions test of aptitude rather than achievement is that it sifts out "diamonds in the rough": bright, promising students who have gone to mediocre high schools but who could flourish at a good college.

This was the rationale of James Bryant Conant, the president of Harvard who in 1934 made the fateful choice to adopt the original SAT for admissions testing of scholarship students, and later persuaded other Ivy League schools to do the same. A self-described "American radical," Conant held that the essence of American democracy was the denial of the doctrine of hereditary privilege. But he was no egalitarian. An ardent believer in Thomas Jefferson's natural aristocracy of virtue and talents, Conant wanted to revolutionize not just Harvard but American education and American society by overthrowing the artificial aristocracy of wealth. (Convinced that genuine equality of opportunity required not just upward but downward mobility, Conant was, in his own phrase, "lusty in wielding the axe against the root of inherited privilege"; to the dismay of many Harvard men, he publicly favored a 100 percent inheritance tax.)

For Conant, it was essential that the scholarship boys who would spearhead the transformation of Harvard into a bastion of the natural elite be chosen without any regard to wealth or family, but solely on the basis of academic merit. And that merit, Conant insisted, could not be accurately measured by achievement tests, because those were manipulable by the rich. Performance on achievement tests is heavily affected by prior preparation and schooling. True merit, Conant held, was basic aptitude or intelligence, because that alone was untainted by artificial privilege. And Conant chose the SAT as his gateway test because he was persuaded that it was a genuine test of aptitude.

[T]he new [SAT] writing test will become an indispensable equalizer. . . .

Contrast Conant's vision of the SAT as the great equalizer of opportunity with the very different reality of the exam today, and particularly the vast and expanding test prep industry. Though the College Board continues to assure parents and students that coaching for the SAT produces only meager gains—on average, just 26 points (out of a possible 1,600) more than the 43-point gain to be expected from simply taking the test again—the public apparently does not believe it. Around $100 million a year, by some estimates, is spent on test preparation materials and services, including those peddled by the College Board itself. . . .

In New York, where the competition to gain entry to elite colleges seems to have reached an unparalleled frenzy, the typical private school student now prepares for the SAT by studying one-on-one with a private tutor. Tutors with a reputation for eliciting significantly higher scores can command fees of hundreds of dollars an hour. The most successful such tutor in the city currently charges $565 for 50 minutes (most tutors get a lot less) and has all the work he can handle. For families who can afford it, total fees to prepare one student for the SAT can amount to several tens of thousands of dollars. (Comparable sums are spent on professional admissions counselors to "package" the student and supervise the applications; the current market leader in New York charges a flat fee of $28,995.) And, despite what the College Board would have people believe is possible, parents are not paying all this for only modest increases. Score gains in the range of 100 to 300 points—enough to make a difference at Princeton or Duke or Berkeley—are expected and more often than not accomplished.

However things may have worked in the past, the reality that higher SAT scores can now readily be bought makes a mockery of the equal-opportunity case for aptitude testing. Conant was wrong: Either the SAT was not and is not an aptitude test, or aptitude tests can be coached for, or both. "Diamonds in the rough" are now more likely to be among the losers, those who cannot afford coaching or who continue to believe the myth that since it is supposed to be an aptitude test, you really cannot study for it.

Competition under the new SAT will be fairer, at least in that everyone will know that the college entrance exam is an achievement test and that the best preparation truly is studying hard in a demanding high school and reading and writing as much as possible. Still, as long as there is unequal access to excellent college preparatory schools, equal opportunity as Conant conceived it will not be realized. Coaching will continue under the new SAT, since parents naturally want to give their children every possible advantage. But by calling attention to the deficiencies of so many public schools, the new test should at least fuel pressure for the reforms (including school choice and vouchers) necessary to rectify or ameliorate them.

Indeed, short of a second Sputnik, it is hard to think of a single event or innovation that could do more to enlist the interested efforts of students, parents, and high schools on behalf of more rigorous standards. When the SAT begins to test writing, especially, parents will insist that schools do much more to teach it, and as a result colleges may soon see fewer freshmen for whom standard written English is practically a foreign language. And at least in one key respect, the new writing test will become an indispensable equalizer: Since application essays nowadays are increasingly edited, if not ghost-written, by professionals, the writing sample will provide colleges with invaluable evidence of exactly what the candidate can do without assistance. All in all, then, the new SAT must be seen as an advance for educational quality and equal opportunity.

12

The New SAT Is Flawed

National Council of Teachers of English

Founded in 1911, the National Council of Teachers of English (NCTE) promotes teaching, research, and student achievement in English at all levels of education. NCTE is based in Urbana, Illinois.

In March 2005, an extensively revised version of the SAT, the SAT Reasoning Test, replaced the previous version due to allegations that it was not a fair or reliable exam. Yet an investigation of the new SAT reveals that the recent changes are flawed and raise new serious concerns. Notably, the new timed essay-writing examination may not be a reliable indicator of writing ability, an accurate predictor of first-year grades, or require writing skill that has instructional value. Furthermore, cultural assumptions of "good" writing can hurt the scores of ethnic students and students who speak English as a second language. Conclusively, the new SAT is fundamentally problematic.

The widespread anxiety that accompanied the first administration of the new SAT exam in March 2005 and the intensive press coverage of the event testify to the important role that the SAT has come to play in American education. This task force [The National Council of Teachers of English] was charged with examining the most extensive change to that test in a decade and perhaps the most important change in the test's history: the addition of a 25-minute timed essay as a

National Council of Teachers of English, *Impact of the SAT and ACT Timed Writing Tests: Report from the NCTE Task Force on SAT and ACT Writing Tests.* Urbana, IL: National Council of Teachers of English, 2005, pp. 1–4, 9–12. Reproduced by permission of the publisher.

required component of the test. Our investigation into this change (and into the timed essay component of the ACT, which is optional) found that many of the concerns about the test that have been expressed in the popular press and in professional forums are warranted. These are serious concerns that speak to the potential of this test to compromise student writers and undermine longstanding efforts to improve writing instruction in the nation's schools. At the same time, the addition of a written component to the SAT and the attention this change has generated provide opportunities for NCTE to bring important questions about the nature of writing instruction to the fore of the ongoing public debates about literacy education in the U.S. . . .

Validity and Reliability

Any writing test will raise questions about validity and reliability. The professional literature is replete with research on these questions as well as critiques of writing tests as valid and reliable means of assessing writing ability. But these longstanding concerns take on added significance in the context of a test of the scale and consequence of the SAT. Because of the scale of the test (taken by 1.4 million students in 2004), and because of its widespread use for college admissions decisions and sometimes for placement into college courses, questions about the test's validity and reliability are magnified. With that context in mind, we make the following points:

a) *Although the College Board [the organization that administers the SAT] has advertised the timed writing component of the SAT as new, the specific format of the SAT timed essay is similar to short, timed, impromptu essay tests that have long been available; it is therefore subject to the same questions that have long been raised about such tests* (see b and d below). Most important, the SAT's timed essay, in its current form, will add little or nothing to what can usefully be determined about a student's writing ability through impromptu writing tests.

b) *Available evidence suggests that scores from this test (or the equivalent one from ACT) will have limited value in decisions about student applicants seeking admission to college.* Studies conducted by the testing firms themselves show that a single, short, impromptu essay adds little or nothing to the predictive power of other measures, such as high school GPA or "verbal proficiency" scores. In a review of four studies conducted by the College Board on the effect of a timed writing component on the predictive validity of the SAT (what is termed "incremental validity"), the largest improvement in predictive validity ranged from .03 to .08; one study showed improvement of zero to .02. The report concludes, "Based on studies of the predictive validity of the SAT II: Writing Test, the new SAT I writing section may be expected to add modestly to the predictive validity of the SAT I". Given these figures, even the term "modest" seems overstated. In short, given the other potential consequences of the addition of a timed writing test to the SAT that we discuss in this report, this very small increase in incremental validity is an extremely weak justification for adding the new writing test.

c) *The predictive validity of a short, impromptu, holistically scored essay is severely limited when it comes to predicting first-year course grades, first-year writing performance, or retention.* By itself, such a score correlates with any of these target variables at about .30, accounting for less than 10 percent of the way students vary on that variable. . . . In short, there is no evidence that the new SAT writing test will be useful in predicting students' first-year course grades, first-year writing performance, or retention.

d) *The kind of writing skill required to do well on short, timed essay tests has little instructional validity.* Given only 25 minutes to write the SAT essay (30 minutes for the ACT essay), students will likely produce a kind of writing that is necessarily formulaic and superficial—writing that is very different from the lengthier, in-depth, and complex writing expected by most college instructors, who tend to discourage rapid, unrevised writing, especially because it encourages rote organization and superficial thinking. One recent study shows how radically the expectations of college composition teachers depart from the writing encouraged by the SAT and ACT exams. (This gap between the SAT essay score and college course may be further widened by the way the essay is scored, because Pearson Educational Measurement, who has been hired by the College Board to rate the essays, does not require their raters to have taught in college; the College Board reports that 58% of its current reader pool teaches at the postsecondary level and 42% at the secondary level.)

e) *The College Board has developed the SAT essay test very quickly, raising further questions about its validity.* Apparently the College Board has run tests of concurrent validity (correlations with previous SAT exams) and internal validity (correlations with other parts of the same examination), though these have nothing necessarily to do with instructional or predictive validity. A high correlation between the new timed writing test and indirect verbal testing would do little more than reinforce the poor validity of the impromptu essay, because historically indirect verbal scores on standardized tests have the same negligible predictability of around .30.

f) *The SAT writing test was developed for the relatively narrow purpose of college admissions decisions and is not appropriate for other purposes.* The College Board states that college admissions officers can use the new essay essentially to verify the authenticity of applicants' personal statements. Such a use of the test is extremely questionable, especially if the applicant is a second-language/second-dialect speaker. The writing of many students often declines in performance under impromptu, timed composing conditions. The College Board also reports on its Web site that 32% of college admissions directors it polled reported plans to use the new SAT writing test for placement purposes. Given that the SAT writing test was neither designed nor validated for these different purposes, these possible uses of the test are cause for concern.

Ultimately, given that so much is riding on these tests and given that their use is likely to grow for purposes beyond college admission, one of the most important questions we need to ask is whether the timed written component of the SAT can measure what the College Board claims it can measure and whether it can do so reliably. We believe that the writing test will be neither valid measure of students' overall writing ability nor a reliable predictor of students' college performance. . . .

Because background knowledge can affect writing quality, students from diverse backgrounds may be disadvantaged by the SAT timed writing test.

Equity and Diversity

Our investigation has also identified several serious issues regarding equity and diversity related to the new timed writing test on the SAT. Specifically, based on available research and our collective experience, we believe that the new timed writing tests have the potential to affect various segments of the national student population disproportionately and to place at a disadvantage students who may already be at risk in various ways:

a) *Some research indicates that teachers in schools with limited resources serving students of lower socioeconomic status have taken a formulaic, lock-step approach to skill development and concept building when faced with high-stakes tests. It seems likely that teachers of such students will respond* defensively to the high-stakes nature of this test by resorting to drills and templates intended to prepare their students to earn high scores. This is not meant as a criticism of teachers who understandably take an efficient and ethical approach to a test that may unfairly disadvantage their students. But as a consequence, these students may experience less effective overall writing instruction, having fewer opportunities to write for authentic purposes to authentic audiences about topics they have some knowledge about.

b) *Students from diverse backgrounds may bring to the new writing tests very different cultural assumptions about writing that may compromise their ability to score well on an impromptu, timed essay that emphasizes a specific conception of "good" writing*, as we noted above. Research shows that such students already tend to believe that they are poor writers at school, in part because the criticisms they receive about their writing focus on standards of form and correctness that may not coincide with their own cultural and linguistic experiences. These standards for "good" writing may differ significantly from the cultural preferences for writing that many students bring to school.

c) *The lack of choice in the timed writing prompts may compromise some students and not others.* Some research indicates that student choice can affect writing quality. In one large-scale study of a statewide writing assessment, researchers found that gender and race, when combined with choice, had an impact on student scores, particularly in the areas of writing conventions and sentence formation (which are emphasized in the SAT writing test); females and Black students tended to write better when given a choice of writing topics.

d) *Because background knowledge can affect writing quality, students from diverse backgrounds may be disadvantaged by the SAT timed writing test.* Students from different racial and ethnic backgrounds may bring different kinds of experiential knowledge to the test situation and may lack the specific knowledge necessary for earning high scores on the SAT timed writing test, which asks students to write about specific topics without supplying information about those topics. For example, the explanations for higher scores on the sample essays on the College Board Web site emphasize the need for supporting evidence. Providing such evidence generally calls for a student not only to draw on the information provided in the test document, but also to draw on background knowledge about the topic, which students from certain cultural backgrounds may not have.

e) *The holistic scoring procedure for the timed writing test may introduce bias that can place students from some background at a disadvantage.* The College Board had described a relatively conventional procedure for rating the essays whereby each essay will be read by two raters, who will use a rubric designed for this purpose. However, even with guidelines for rating the essays, individual raters can lack sensitivity to and knowledge about the characteristic features of students' vernacular languages. . . .

f) *The concerns expressed here may be exacerbated for second-language and second-dialect learners, who may lack the implicit language knowledge to enable them to negotiate impromptu writing tasks quickly and effectively.*

g) *The increased cost of the new SAT may cause hardship for students of limited economic means.* Although the College Board claims that scholarships or fee waivers are available for students who cannot afford the cost of the test, we find it hard to believe that all such students will be identified and assisted by this program. It is likely that some students may exempt themselves from the test because of the costs. In addition, students of limited economic means will likely not have access to test preparation resources available to more privileged students.

Worsening the Gap

The College Board itself has recently studied the impact of different writing prompts on the new test, concluding, "Results of the impact analyses revealed no significant prompt type effects for ethnic, gender, or language groups, although there were significant differences in mean scores for ethnic and gender groups for all prompts". In the study, African American and Hispanic students scored significantly lower than their White and Asian American counterparts on all tested prompts, suggesting, as we have noted above, continued inequities in these tests related to racial and/or ethnic background. (It should be noted that all tested writing prompts in this study conformed to the general format and nature of the kind of sample writing prompts provided by the College Board on its Web site. In other words, the kind of writing encouraged by these tested prompts was essentially the same for all the prompts; therefore, the concerns we have raised about the limitations of these short, impromptu writing tests apply to all the prompts used in the study. Given the similarity of the tested prompts, it is not surprising that differences in performance among students of different racial and ethnic backgrounds were consistent across the different writing prompts. Nevertheless, in its overview of its own research, the College Board claims that "the results of this study indicated that the essay prompt type that will be used on the new SAT did not disadvantage any particular group of students." Technically, that's correct, but it's also misleading, since students of different groups performed differently on all tested prompts.)

In short, our review indicates that the timed writing tests may worsen the gap in educational preparedness between the nation's "haves" and "have nots."

13

Assessment Through Standardized Testing Is Recommended for Colleges

U.S. Department of Education Commission on the Future of Higher Education

The Commission on the Future of Higher Education is a nineteen-member government agency formed by U.S. Secretary of Education Margaret Spellings in 2005. Its aim is to form strategies to improve access and affordability of higher education and raise educational standards and accountability of U.S. colleges and universities.

While higher education systems in other nations are making strides, higher education in the United States, in several areas, falls short of adequacy and is even on the decline. This disturbing evidence makes a compelling case for assessing college student achievement and postsecondary institution accountability through standardized testing. Assessment is important to the identification of shortcomings in curricula and classroom instruction, measurement of student progress, and raising of higher education standards, which will better prepare young Americans for the global workplace of the twenty-first century.

As other nations rapidly improve their higher education systems, we are disturbed by evidence that the quality of student learning at U.S. colleges and universities is inadequate and, in some cases, declining. A number of recent studies

U.S. Department of Education, Commission on the Future of Higher Education, *A Test of Leadership: Charting the Future of U.S. Higher Education*. Washington, D.C.: Ed Pubs, 2006, pp. 3–4, 13, 23–24. Reproduced by permission.

highlight the shortcomings of postsecondary institutions in everything from graduation rates and time to degree to learning outcomes and even core literacy skills. According to the most recent National Assessment of Adult Literacy, for instance, the percentage of college graduates deemed proficient in prose literacy has actually declined from 40 to 31 percent in the past decade. These shortcomings have real-world consequences. Employers report repeatedly that many new graduates they hire are not prepared to work, lacking the critical thinking, writing and problem-solving skills needed in today's workplaces. In addition, business and government leaders have repeatedly and urgently called for workers at all stages of life to continually upgrade their academic and practical skills. But both national and state policies and the practices of postsecondary institutions have not always made this easy, by failing to provide financial and logistical support for lifelong learning and by failing to craft flexible credit-transfer systems that allow students to move easily between different kinds of institutions. . . .

Findings Regarding Learning

At a time when we need to be increasing the quality of learning outcomes and the economic value of a college education, there are disturbing signs that suggest we are moving in the opposite direction. As a result, the continued ability of American postsecondary institutions to produce informed and skilled citizens who are able to lead and compete in the 21st-century global marketplace may soon be in question.

We have slipped to 12th in higher education attainment.

- While U.S. higher education has long been admired internationally, our continued preeminence is no longer something we can take for granted. The rest of the world is catching up, and by some measures has already overtaken us. We have slipped to 12th in higher education attainment and 16th in high school graduation rates.

• While educators and policymakers have commendably focused on getting more students into college, too little attention has been paid to helping them graduate. The result is that unacceptable numbers of students fail to complete their studies at all, while even those that graduate don't always learn enough. Several national studies highlight shortcomings in the quality of U.S. higher education as measured by literacy, rising time to degree, and disturbing racial and ethnic gaps in student achievement:

> The National Assessment of Adult Literacy indicates that, between 1992 and 2003, average prose literacy (the ability to understand narrative texts such as newspaper articles) decreased for all levels of educational attainment, and document literacy (the ability to understand practical information such as instructions for taking medicine) decreased among those with at least some college education or a bachelor's degree or higher.

> Only 66 percent of full-time four-year college students complete a baccalaureate degree within six years. (This reflects the percentage of students who begin full-time in four-year institutions and graduate within six years.)

> Significant attainment gaps between white and Asian students and black and Hispanic students remain during the college years.

> Employers complain that many college graduates are not prepared for the workplace and lack the new set of skills necessary for successful employment and continuous career development. . . .

Recommendations

- Higher education institutions should measure student learning using quality-assessment data from instruments such as, for example, the Collegiate Learning Assessment, which measures the growth of student learning taking place in colleges, and the Measure of Academic Proficiency and Progress, which is designed to assess general education outcomes for undergraduates in order to improve the quality of instruction and learning.

- The federal government should provide incentives for states, higher education associations, university systems, and institutions to develop interoperable outcomes-focused accountability systems designed to be accessible and useful for students, policymakers, and the public, as well as for internal management and institutional improvement.

- Faculty must be at the forefront of defining educational objectives for students and developing meaningful, evidence-based measures of their progress toward those goals.

- The results of student learning assessments, including value-added measurements that indicate how students' skills have improved over time, should be made available to students and reported in the aggregate publicly. Higher education institutions should make aggregate summary results of all postsecondary learning measures, e.g., test scores, certification and licensure attainment, time to degree, graduation rates, and other relevant measures, publicly available in a consumer-friendly form as a condition of accreditation.

- The collection of data from public institutions allowing meaningful interstate comparison of student learning should be encouraged and implemented in all states. By using assessments of adult literacy, licensure, graduate and professional school exams, and specially administered tests of general intellectual skills, state policymakers can make valid interstate comparisons of student learning and identify shortcomings as well as best practices. The federal government should provide financial support for this initiative. . . .

Examples of Student Learning Assessments

The Collegiate Learning Assessment: Among the most comprehensive national efforts to measure how much students actually learn at different campuses, the Collegiate Learning Assessment (CLA) promotes a culture of evidence-based assessment in higher education. Since 2002, 134 colleges and universities have used the exam, which evaluates students' critical thinking, analytic reasoning, and written communication using performance tasks and writing prompts rather than multiple choice questions. Administered to freshmen and seniors, the CLA allows for comparability to national norms and measurement of value added between the freshman and senior years. Additionally, because the CLA's unit of analysis is the institution and not the student, results are aggregated and allow for inter-institutional comparisons that show how each institution contributes to learning.

The **National Survey of Student Engagement and the Community College Survey of Student Engagement**: Administered by the Indiana University Center for Postsecondary Research, the National Survey of Student Engagement (NSSE) and its community college counterpart, the Community College Survey of Student Engagement (CCSSE), survey hundreds of institutions annually about student participation and engagement in programs designed to improve their learning and development. The measures of student engagement—the time and effort students put into educational activities in and out of the classroom, from meeting with professors to reading books that weren't assigned in class—serve as a proxy for the value and quality of their undergraduate experience NSSE and CCSSE provide colleges and universities with readily usable data to improve that experience and create benchmarks against which similar institutions can compare themselves. With surveys from several million students already compiled, these instruments provide a comprehensive picture of the undergraduate student experience at four-year and two-year institutions. Results from NSSE and CCSSE, which are publicly reported, can provide institutions and external stakeholders data for improving institutional performance, setting accountability standards, and strategic planning.

The National Forum on College-Level Learning: The National Forum on College-Level Learning has been called "the first attempt to measure what the college educated know and can do across states" Piloted in 2002 across Illinois, Kentucky, Nevada, Oklahoma, and South Carolina, the study collected data on student learning using multiple assessment instruments already in use or widely available such as the National Adult Literacy Survey, the Collegiate Learning Assessment (for four-year colleges) or WorkKeys (for two-year colleges), and graduate admissions exams. Results from these assessments provide states comparable information on how their colleges and universities contribute to student learning and identify challenges such as performance gaps and inconsistent teacher preparation. Comparable assessment also allows states to identify best practices, providing information useful in creating policy and programs that will improve the states' intellectual capital.

14

Assessment Through Standardized Testing Isn't Recommended for Colleges

Shai D. Bronshtein

Shai D. Bronshtein is an undergraduate in social studies at Harvard University and an editor at the Harvard Crimson, *the country's oldest daily college newspaper in continuous circulation.*

To hold universities accountable for the so-called quality of their education, the U.S. Department of Education Commission for the Future of Higher Education proposes that college students' achievement and progress be assessed through standardized testing. Such a strategy is counterproductive and should not take place at the collegiate level. Middle and high schools—not postsecondary institutions—should be accountable for the achievement gaps in literacy and math. Standardized testing in college is redundant because accountability is already assessed through accreditation. Furthermore, mandatory nationwide testing would place unconstitutional limits on what is taught and ways of teaching at the nation's diverse range of colleges and universities.

The Commission on the Future of Higher Education recently recommended that colleges begin mandating standardized tests for students, in order to supposedly hold universities and educators responsible for the education they purport to provide. However, as far as higher education is concerned, the last thing that is necessary is some form of standardized testing.

Shai D. Bronshtein, "Standardization Without Reason," *Harvard Crimson*, April 3, 2006. Reproduced by permission.

A standardized educational curriculum is mandated through high school. This is the timeframe in which states are required to provide students the basic skills they need to be "productive" members of society. If the states cannot teach children basic algebra and other essential skills in 12 or sometimes 13 years, why should the burden fall to universities? Standardized testing already exists in high schools thanks to illegitimate, improper federal bullying such as the No Child Left Behind Act. This practice, imposing a national standardized education curriculum, is improper at the high school level, let alone at the college level.

Not only is college completely optional education, it is also a time of specialization for those who attend. Many students go to college to learn a particular skill; most colleges require students to major in one specific field or another. How can one expect a music concentrator to have the same strengths as a biology concentrator? To satisfy these national education requirements, colleges would have to completely alter their educational philosophies.

Furthermore, standardized tests in general are an enormous waste of time and money. Students waste countless hours in the standardized testing process; whether the hours spent include learning content specifically (and only) because it is found on the test, or the several hours spent taking the test itself, time is thrown way on an incredibly arbitrary "validation" of what one should already know.

Some argue that this time is well-spent, that we should always hold students and professors and even institutions accountable for the education that should be accrued. A multiple-choice test, however, cannot accurately assess true knowledge of a subject, and some students have difficulty showing what they know in a standardized test format. There are countless stories of students improving 200 or more points on the SAT, either with or without extra preparation. According to the logic of standardized tests, this means that these students are 12.5 percent smarter than before the course, that they have gained immense knowledge from practicing analogies repeatedly. This, however, seems improbable. In many ways, knowledge cannot be measured by filling in bubbles for three hours—especially in the humanities and social sciences.

Inherently Flawed and Redundant

Even ignoring the fact that the tests are inherently flawed, they are also simply redundant, the means to measure accountability already exists through the process of accreditation. This process, which is carried out at pre-ordained intervals by a regional governing board, is supposed to evaluate whether an academic institution is indeed academically institutionalized enough. If a school has accreditation, it has already passed the tests and has been certified as a valid educational center.

Even more basically, every state has an interest in ensuring that its colleges and universities are performing and educating their students. A state with schools that are failing will have a vested interest in fixing these schools because educated citizens and workers make the state stronger, there is no reason for the federal government to get involved unless states ask for help.

When considering standardized testing at the collegiate level, it is impossible to see it as anything but wasteful, without merit, and disregarding the spirit of the Constitution.

These regulations even usher in the threat of censorship. Many universities have unorthodox views, whether very conservative or very liberal, or even completely off the political spectrum. If the federal government imposes a curriculum, which is essentially what standardized testing does, it will limit the way schools can teach and even what they are allowed to teach because they will have to pander to the arbitrary, supposedly neutral and politically correct standards of some national education advisory committee.

It would be difficult for the government to dictate that private universities use standardized testing because this would clearly violate basic constitutional limitations on federal power, simply put, Congress does not have the right to impose arbitrary standards on non-essential, private educational institutions. At best, it is a state's right to address this issue. Recognizing this, the plan suggests rescinding federal financial aid from students who go to universities that do not adopt standardized testing practices. By coercing schools into adopting these tests, the government would be skirting the constitutionality issue while showing utter contempt for the spirit of the document.

For many students, college education is an entirely private matter, undertaken with their own funds for their own purposes. The government has no justification for testing these students because they get no money from the government. Everyone in such situations who does not receive individual financial aid would still have to take the tests but would receive no direct benefit from them. These unfortunate students would essentially be paying for "justification" of their private education while receiving no tangible benefits in the form of federal aid or a measurably better or more comprehensive education.

When considering standardized testing at the collegiate level, it is impossible to see it as anything but wasteful, without merit, and disregarding the Spirit of the Constitution. It should not be implemented under the current educational system, and hopefully Congress will have the wisdom to ignore the recommendations of the Committee on the Future of Higher Education.

Organizations to Contact

The editors have compiled the following list of organizations concerned with the issues debated in this book. The descriptions are derived from materials provided by the organizations. All have publications or information available for interested readers. The list was compiled on the date of publication of the present volume; the information provided here may change. Be aware that many organizations take several weeks or longer to respond to inquiries, so allow as much time as possible.

American Federation of Teachers
555 New Jersey Avenue, NW, Washington, DC   20001
(202) 879-4400
Web site: www.aft.org

The American Federation of Teachers (AFT) was founded in 1916 to represent the economic, social, and professional interests of classroom teachers. It has more than three thousand local affiliates nationwide, forty-three state affiliates, and more than 1.3 million members. It publishes the *PSRP Reporter*, a quarterly newsletter.

The Carnegie Foundation for the Advancement of Teaching
51 Vista Lane, Stanford, CA   94305
(650) 566-5100 • fax: (650) 326-0278
Web site: www.carnegiefoundation.org

Established in 1905, the Carnegie Foundation is an independent policy and research center that specializes in teaching. Its program areas include K-12, undergraduate, graduate, and professional education. It produces many publications, including the higher-education-centered *Change* magazine.

The College Board
45 Columbus Avenue, New York, NY   10023
Web site: www.collegeboard.com

The College Board is a not-for-profit membership association whose mission is to connect students to college success and opportunity. It is composed of more than 5,200 schools, colleges, universities, and other educational organizations. Its programs include the SAT Reasoning Test, the *Preliminary SAT/National Merit Scholarship Qualifying Test* (PSAT/NMSQT), and the Advanced Placement Program (AP).

Educational Testing Service (ETS)
Rosedale Road, Princeton, NJ   08541
(609) 921-9000 • fax: (609) 734-5410
Web site: www.ets.org

Educational Testing Service (ETS) is a testing and assessment organization which administers the SAT Reasoning Test, *Preliminary SAT/National Merit Scholarship Qualifying Test* (PSAT/NMSQT), Graduate Record Examination (GRE), and *Test Of English as a Foreign Language* (TOEFL).

National Center for Fair and Open Testing
342 Broadway, Cambridge, MA   02139
(617) 864-4810 • fax: (617) 497-2224
Web site: www.fairtest.org

National Center for Fair and Open Testing, or FairTest, is an organization that advocates for the reform of current standardized testing and assessment practices in education and employment. It publishes a regular electronic newsletter, the *Examiner*, plus a full catalog of materials on both K-12 and university testing to aid teachers, administrators, students, parents, and researchers.

National Council of Teachers of English
1111 W. Kenyon Road, Urbana, IL   61801-1096
(877) 369-6283 • fax: (217) 328-9645
Web site: www.ncte.org

Founded in 1911, the National Council of Teachers of English (NCTE) promotes teaching, research, and student achievement in English language and literature at all levels of education.

The council published the report, *The Impact of the SAT and ACT Timed Writing Tests,* which raises serious concerns about the revised version of the SAT.

National Education Association
1201 16th Street, NW, Washington, DC   20036-3290
(202) 833-4000
Web site: www.nea.org

The National Education Association (NEA) is a volunteer-based organization that represents 3.2 million public school teachers, university and college faculty members, college students training to be teachers, retired educators, and other educational professionals. It has affiliate organizations in every state and publishes an electronic newsletter.

Public Agenda
6 East 39th Street, 9th Floor, New York, NY   10016
(212) 686-6610 • fax: (212) 889-3461
Web site: www.publicagenda.org

Public Agenda is a nonpartisan organization that researches public opinion and produces informational materials on policy issues. Its reports on standardized testing include *Reality Check 2006: Is Support for Standards and Testing Fading?* and *Survey Finds Little Sign of Backlash Against Academic Standards or Standardized Tests.*

U.S. Department of Education
400 Maryland Avenue, SW, Washington, DC   20202
(800) USA-LEARN (872-5327)
Web site: www.ed.gov

The U.S. Department of Education was created in 1980 by combining offices from several federal agencies. The Department's mission is to promote student achievement and preparation for global competitiveness by fostering educational excellence and ensuring equal access.

Bibliography

Books

Frederick M. Hess and Michael J. Petrilli *No Child Left Behind Primer.* New York: Peter Lang Publishing, 2006.

Jerome Karabel *The Chosen: The Hidden History of Admission and Exclusion at Harvard, Yale, and Princeton.* Boston: Houghton Mifflin, 2005.

Alfie Kohn *What Does it Mean to Be Well Educated? And More Essays on Standards, Grading, and Other Follies.* Boston: Beacon Press, 2004.

Deborah Meier and George Wood, eds. *Many Children Left Behind: How the No Child Left Behind Act Is Damaging Our Children and Our Schools.* Boston: Beacon Press, 2004.

Richard P. Phelps, ed. *Defending Standardized Testing.* Mahwah, NJ: L. Erlbaum Associates, 2005.

Richard P. Phelps *Kill the Messenger: The War on Standardized Testing.* New Brunswick, NJ: Transaction Publishers, 2003.

Peter Sacks *Standardized Minds: The High Price of America's Testing Culture and What We Can Do to Change It.* New York: Perseus Publishing, 2001.

Decker F. Walker and Jonas F. Soltis *Curriculum and Aims,* 4th ed. New York: Teachers College Press, 2004.

Rebecca Zwick   *Rethinking the SAT: The Future of Standardized Testing in University Admissions.* New York: Routledge-Falmer, 2004.

Periodicals

Karen W. Arenson and Diana B. Henriques   "Company's Errors on SAT Scores Raise New Qualms About Testing," *New York Times*, March 10, 2006.

Dan Brown   "What We Learned in School This Year," *Huffington Post*, June 26, 2007.

John Buell   "No Child Left Behind Still Fails," *Reno Gazette-Journal*, June 21, 2007.

Carl K. Chafin   "Using Student Performance Data Humanely: The Danger of Losing Perspective on Teaching and Learning and the Value of Test Scores," *School Administrator*, December 2004.

Chicago Sun-Times   "Standardized Tests, Uniformity: None of the Above for Colleges," February 21, 2006.

Joanne V. Creighton   "It Doesn't Test for Success," *Los Angeles Times*, March 13, 2006.

Allen Desoff   "NCLB's Purity: Flaws Notwithstanding, No Child Left Behind Has Brought About Significant Academic Improvement and Is Here to Stay," *District Administration*, November 2006.

Michael Dobbs   "New SAT a Boon for Test-Prep Business," *Washington Post*, March 7, 2005.

Jay P. Greene and Marcus A. Winters   "California Should End Social Promotion," *San Diego Union-Tribune*, December 9, 2004.

Eric Hoover   "Testing 1, 2, 3," *Chronicle of Higher Education*, January 6, 2006.

Patrick Kennedy   "Breaking the No. 2 Pencil: The Case for Abolishing Standardized Tests," *Johns Hopkins News-Letter*, April 6, 2006.

Herb Ladley   "Bringing Merit Back," *Cavalier Daily*, July 21, 2005.

Jay Mathews   "Test Wars," *Newsweek*, August 21, 2006.

Monty Neill and Lisa Guisbond   "Rethink Standardized Tests," *USA Today*, December 14, 2004.

Amanda Paulson   "What Happens When Teachers Fail the Test," *Christian Science Monitor*, August 15, 2003.

Anna Quindlen   "Testing: One, Two, Three," *Newsweek*, June 13, 2005.

Leslie Raybum   "The Standardized Classroom," *World and I*, June 2003.

Paige Rod	"Q: Are the Tests Required by No Child Left Behind Making Schools More Accountable? Yes: Testing Has Raised Students' Expectations, and Progress in Learning Is Evident Nationwide," *Insight on the News*, May 11, 2004.
Fredreka Schouten	"Standardized Tests Take on Shades of Gray," *USA Today*, June 28, 2004.
Claude M. Steele	"Not Just a Test," *Nation*, May 3, 2004.
Claudia Wallis and Sonja Steptoe	"How to Fix No Child Left Behind," *Time*, May 24, 2007.

Index